This book must be returned immediately
⋯r b⋯ the Librarian, and in
⋯ stamp⋯

D1614724

American Rhetoric
and the
Vietnam War

AMERICAN RHETORIC
AND THE
VIETNAM WAR

J. Justin Gustainis

Praeger Series in Political Communication

Westport, Connecticut
London

Library of Congress Cataloging-in-Publication Data

Gustainis, J. Justin.
    American rhetoric and the Vietnam War / J. Justin Gustainis.
        p.   cm.—(Praeger series in political communication, ISSN
    1062–5623)
        Includes bibliographical references and index.
        ISBN 0–275–93361–X (alk. paper)
        1. Vietnamese Conflict, 1961–1975—Propaganda.   2. Vietnamese
    Conflict, 1961–1975—Protests movements—United States.
    3. Vietnamese Conflict, 1961–1975, in mass media—United States.
    4. United States—Politics and government—1945–   I. Title.
    II. Series.
    DS559.8.P65G87   1993
    959.704'3373—dc20   92–36553

British Library Cataloguing in Publication Data is available.

Library of Congress Catalog Card Number: 92–36553
ISBN: 0–275–93361–X
ISSN: 1062–5623

First published in 1993

Praeger Publishers, 88 Post Road West, Westport, CT 06881
An imprint of Greenwood Publishing Group, Inc.

Printed in the United States of America

The paper used in this book complies with the Permanent
Paper Standard issued by the National Information Standards
Organization (Z39.48–1984).

10   9   8   7   6   5   4   3   2   1

Copyright Acknowledgments

The author gratefully acknowledges permission to quote from the following sources:

J. Justin Gustainis, "John F. Kennedy and the Green Berets: the Rhetorical Use of the
Hero Myth," *Communication Studies* 40 (Spring, 1989), pp. 41–53.

J. Justin Gustainis and Dan F. Hahn, "While the Whole World Watched: Rhetorical
Failures of Anti-War Protest," *Communication Quarterly* 36/3 (Summer, 1988), pp. 203–
216.

J. Justin Gustainis, " 'Waist Deep in the Big Muddy': Rhetorical Dimensions of the Tet
Offensive." From *Political Communication and Persuasion*, 5, 1988, pp. 81–92. PA: Crane
Russak and Company. Used with permission.

DOONESBURY copyright G. B. Trudeau. Reprinted with permission of UNIVERSAL
PRESS SYNDICATE. All rights reserved.

In memory of my parents:

Austin S. Gustainis
(1910–1975)

Eleanor E. Gustainis
(1909–1991)

Contents

Series Foreword

Those of us from the discipline of communication studies have long believed that communication is prior to all other fields of inquiry. In several other forums, I have argued that the essence of politics is "talk" or human interaction.[1] Such interaction may be formal or informal, verbal or nonverbal, public or private, but it is always persuasive, forcing us consciously or subconsciously to interpret, to evaluate, and to act. Communication is the vehicle for human action.

From this perspective, it is not surprising that Aristotle recognized the natural kinship of politics and communication in his writings *Politics* and *Rhetoric*. In the former, he establishes that humans are "political beings [who] alone of the animals [are] furnished with the faculty of language.[2] And in the latter, he begins his systematic analysis of discourse by proclaiming that "rhetorical study, in its strict sense, is concerned with the modes of persuasion."[3] Thus, it was recognized more than twenty-three hundred years ago that politics and communication go hand in hand because they are essential parts of human nature.

Back in 1981, Dan Nimmo and Keith Sanders proclaimed that political communication was an emerging field.[4] Although its origin, as noted, dates back centuries, a "self-consciously cross-disciplinary" focus began in the late 1950s. Thousands of books and articles later, colleges and universities offer a variety of graduate and undergraduate course work in the area in such diverse departments as communication, mass communication, journalism, political science, and sociology.[5] In Nimmo and Sanders' early assessment, the "key areas of inquiry" included rhetorical analysis, propaganda analysis, attitude change studies, voting studies, government and the news media, functional and systems analyses, technological changes, media technologies, campaign techniques, and re-search techniques.[6] In a survey of the state of the field in 1983, the same authors and Lynda Kaid found additional, more specific areas of con-cerns such as the presidency, political polls, public opinion, debates, and advertising, to name a few.[7] Since the first study, they also noted a shift away from the rather strict behavioral approach.

A decade later, Dan Nimmo and David Swanson argued that "political communication has developed some identity as a more or less distinct domain of scholarly work."[8] The scope and concerns of the area have further expanded to include critical theories and cultural studies. While there is no precise definition, method, or disciplinary home of the area of inquiry, its primary domain is the role, processes, and effects of communication within the context of politics broadly defined.

In 1985, the editors of *Political Communication Yearbook: 1984* noted that "more things are happening in the study, teaching, and practice of political communication than can be captured within the space limita-tions of the relatively few publications available."[9] In addition, they argued that the backgrounds of "those" involved in the field [are] so varied and pluralist in outlook and approach, . . . it [is] a mistake to adhere slavishly to any set format in shaping the content."[10] And more recently, Swanson and Nimmo called for "ways of overcoming the un-happy consequences of fragmentation within a framework that respects, encourages, and benefits from diverse scholarly commitments, agendas, and approaches."[11]

In agreement with these assessments of the area and with gentle encouragement, Praeger established in 1988 the series entitled "Praeger Studies in Political Communication." The series is open to all qualitative and quantitative methodologies as well as contemporary and historical studies. The key to characterizing the studies in the series is the focus on communication variables or activities within a political context or dimension. As of this writing, more than thirty volumes have been published and numerous impressive works are forthcoming. Scholars from the disciplines of communication, history, journalism, political sci-ence, and sociology have participated in the series.

Justin Gustainis provides one of the most comprehensive analyses of the rhetoric of the Vietnam War. For a generation of Americans, Vietnam was always with us, preoccupying our youth and influencing our views of domestic politics and foreign policy. For nearly thirty years, we have struggled with the legacy of the Vietnam War: humiliation of defeat, haunting questions of national purpose, loss of national pride, and gen-eral distrust of government. No less than five American presidents made policy decisions that contributed to our involvement in the conflict. Each created his own illusions of mission, hope, and victory.

Much of the politics of the Reagan era was a direct attempt to confront, redefine, and overcome the lingering effects of the Vietnam War, which culminated in the Persian Gulf War. Reagan told us that our involvement was justified but poorly executed, that those who served were heroes, not criminals, and that our failure was a product of poor leadership, not a lack of the "American will." The celebrations of the short and brief Desert Storm "victory" became a national catharsis of expressions of regret and gratitude for those who served in Vietnam. America, at last, had "won" another "war."

Each chapter in this volume serves as a "mini-study" of the role of rhetoric and a person, a place, a group, an event, or an idea. Within the groupings of prowar rhetoric, antiwar rhetoric, and the rhetoric of the media, Gustainis provides an impressive breadth of topics, concepts, analyses, and methodologies. American rhetoric of the Vietnam War was rich, heroic, tragic, mythic, symbolic, strategic, and even paradoxical. The rhetoric often sought to define us, our actions, and our enemy. Some of the rhetoric sought to inspire us, to sustain us, and to divide us. Much of the rhetoric sought to interpret the past, to define the present, and to predict the future.

This book is an important contribution to the study of rhetoric and of the Vietnam era. It is a valuable addition to the growing works in our field that demonstrates the power and importance of public discourse in American politics. But perhaps most important, this volume provides insight into that still haunting and nagging question of "Why Vietnam?"

I am, without shame or modesty, a fan of the series. The joy of serving as its editor is in participating in the dialogue of the field of political communication and in reading the contributors' works. I invite you to join me.

Robert E. Denton, Jr.

NOTES

1. See Robert E. Denton, Jr., *The Symbolic Dimensions of the American Presidency* (Prospect Heights, IL: Waveland Press, 1982); Robert E. Denton, Jr., and Gary Woodward, *Political Communication in America* (New York: Praeger, 1985; 2d ed., 1990); Robert E. Denton, Jr., and Dan Hahn, *Presidential Communication* (New York: Praeger, 1986); and Robert E. Denton, Jr., *The Primetime Presidency of Ronald Reagan* (New York: Praeger, 1988).

2. Aristotle, *The Politics of Aristotle*, trans. Ernest Barker (New York: Oxford University Press, 1970), 5.

3. Aristotle, *Rhetoric*, trans. Rhys Roberts (New York: The Modern Library, 1954), 22.

4. Dan Nimmo and Keith Sanders, "Introduction: The Emergence of Political Communication as a Field," in *Handbook of Political Communication*, ed. Dan Nimmo and Keith Sanders (Beverly Hills, CA: Sage, 1981), 11–36.

5. Ibid., 15.

6. Ibid., 17–27.

7. Keith Sanders, Lynda Kaid, and Dan Nimmo, eds. *Political Communication Yearbook: 1984* (Carbondale, IL: Southern Illinois University: 1985), 283–308.

8. Dan Nimmo and David Swanson, "The Field of Political Communication: Beyond the Voter Persuasion Paradigm," in *New Directions in Political Communication*, ed. David Swanson and Dan Nimmo (Beverly Hills, CA: Sage, 1990), 8.

9. Sanders, Kaid, and Nimmo, xiv.

10. Ibid., xiv.

11. Nimmo and Swanson, 11.

Acknowledgments

A book like this cannot be written without a great deal of help, and I was fortunate to receive kindness, assistance, and expertise from many people.

I owe thanks to Robert Denton for encouraging me to develop an idea into a book proposal and for recommending that proposal to Praeger. For her incredible patience with my somewhat flexible approach to deadlines, along with her willingness to answer innumerable stupid questions without once characterizing them as such, Anne Kiefer of Praeger Publishers deserves beatification, if not outright sainthood.

The staff of SUNY–Plattsburgh's Feinberg Library, with their usual combination of patience, professionalism, and cheerfulness, made a difficult research task easier. I offer special thanks to reference librarians Tim Hartnett, Carla List, Mike Miranda, and Gordon Muir, and to interlibrary loan librarians Craig Koste and Mary Turner.

I owe a great deal to Dan Hahn of Florida Atlantic University. He cowrote Chapter 8 with me and has taught me a great deal about research and writing through partnership in numerous other projects over the last twelve years. His example continues to inspire me; I want to be just like him when I grow up. I also wish to thank Martha Solomon of the University of Maryland for an excellent criticism of Chapter 2 during its first incarnation as a convention paper.

A number of my students at SUNY–Plattsburgh have provided valuable research assistance and saved me countless hours in the process. Tahnya Laveck found excellent material on SDS for Chapter 6; Sue Ritty delved into the dark world of Weathermen writings for Chapter 7; James Sullivan wrote a paper that provided the inspiration for Chapter 1 and did extra research to help me understand the domino theory; Susan Conner, who was my "research wretch" for three semesters, found valuable material for several of the chapters.

In addition, I want to thank Jacquelyn Connelly for helping me overcome writer's block; Donald Enholm of Bowling Green State University for teaching me most of what I know about rhetoric; and my late parents for teaching me most of what I know about life.

Deborah Wilson, department secretary *extraordinaire*, went above and beyond the call of duty many times in the preparation of the manuscript and did so with unfailing good humor. Special thanks are due to her.

Finally, I give thanks to (and for) my wife, Pat Grogan. She nurtured me, sustained me, and, on several different occasions, talked me out of giving up. Also, thanks to Terry Bear for seeing to my nutritional needs over the years.

Introduction

Vietnam was America's longest war. For that reason, among others, it was also the nation's most controversial war in this century. Public controversy gives rise to public rhetoric as surely as the sparks fly upward, and this may help to explain why the Vietnam War was the stimulus for so much rhetoric, with so much passion, by so many people, for so many years.

Rhetoric during wartime is about the creation of consensus. Since wars tend to drag on, consensus among the citizenry is vital if victory is to be achieved. The citizens of a nation at war are usually asked to sacrifice greatly; they are expected to give their money, their sons, and perhaps even themselves. At minimum, they are required to endure inconvenience; in the extreme, they are asked to die. People in large numbers will agree to do these things only if they believe their cause to be just and their eventual victory to be assured. The best example of wartime consensus in this country took place during World War II. The Japanese attack on Pearl Harbor convinced Americans that war was necessary, and they believed, not without reason, that their population and industrial might would eventually carry the day.

Vietnam was another matter. American involvement in that Southeast Asian nation's affairs began so inconspicuously and increased so gradually, until 1964, that little consensus was called for, at first. Dwight Eisenhower's sending a few hundred advisers was barely noticed by most of the public. John Kennedy's commitment was somewhat greater, but the cost, both in dollars and lives, remained low. Kennedy's claim that a few hundred highly trained guerrilla warfare experts (the much-

heralded Green Berets) could do the job was accepted with few dissenting voices from his constituents.

In the Johnson administration, the spectre of war in Vietnam ceased
to be a speck hovering over a distant horizon and began to loom right
in America's face. Lyndon Johnson, convinced that the nation's vital
interests and international prestige were at stake, increased American
military involvement, and he did so to a level that few could fail to
notice. The creation of consensus was begun in earnest, and its most
conspicuous example involved the Gulf of Tonkin incident and the epon-
ymous resolution that followed. This is where the problems really began.
There began to appear some disagreement, mostly from the Left, about
the place of Southeast Asia among the hierarchy of America's vital interests. Later, questions would be raised concerning the validity of the
Johnson administration's depictions of certain events in Vietnam, including what actually did or did not take place in the Gulf of Tonkin.
Still later, once major military involvement was a reality, doubt arose in
some quarters as to the possibility of the United States achieving all, or
any, of its stated military and political goals.

Although Johnson was fairly successful—mostly by waving the red
flag of Communist aggression—in building and maintaining a consensus
that victory in Vietnam was desirable, he was unable to overcome growing doubts that his policies would achieve that victory. A "credibility
gap" had developed—a chasm between what Johnson said about the
war and what many Americans believed to be true—and he fell into it.

Richard Nixon inherited his predecessors' war and the lack of widespread belief that total victory was possible. Nixon never planned to
"win" in Vietnam. Rather, he intended to negotiate a peace settlement
with North Vietnam that would reflect favorably on his country and his
administration. Thus, the creation of a new consensus was called for—
this one in support of Nixon's policy of "Vietnamization." Meanwhile,
those who failed to share the president's views on the war remained
large in number and loud of voice. Both the number of protesters and
the volume of their protest surged after Nixon ordered a brief military
incursion into neutral Cambodia in the spring of 1970.

This book is about the efforts of several administrations to build consensus about Vietnam and about the failure of those efforts. It is, as the
title indicates, a book about American rhetoric. This is not a denigration
of the importance of rhetoric that arose in other nations, but rather is a
recognition that, in many respects, the war was America's war. The
conflict was largely a product of American culture and values, and it
has had an effect on that culture and those values that has yet to be
completely understood.

My operational definition of "rhetoric" in this work has been quite
broad. I am inclined to regard rhetoric as the deliberate use of symbols

to persuade, and such a wide perspective naturally includes many different types of activity: speeches, of course, but also marches, songs, military campaigns (in some cases), gestures, destruction of property, comic strips, and films.

I do not claim to have written a comprehensive study of the important rhetoric generated in this country by the Vietnam War. A far larger volume than this one—more likely, a series of volumes—would be necessary to accomplish such a task. I have tried instead to discuss some topics that I believe to be significant in the effort to create or dissipate consensus during (and, in the case of films, after) the conflict.

For the sake of balance, I have devoted sections of the book to rhetoric in support of the war, rhetoric opposed to the war, and some depictions of the war that were presented to the nation through the mass media. Much more can be written about the Vietnam War and its rhetoric. There are lessons yet to be learned about the building of consensus, and of the consequences for a nation when the basis for agreement is a combination of wishful thinking and deliberate deception. If I may rephrase some famous words of philosopher George Santayana, those who do not learn the lessons of Vietnam are doomed to repeat them.

Part One

Prowar Rhetoric

Chapter One

Dangerous Metaphor: The Domino Theory as Condensation Symbol

In early April 1954, as the Communist Viet Minh were slowly but inevitably tightening the noose around the French garrison at Dien Bien Phu, President Dwight Eisenhower held his regularly scheduled news conference. Most of the questions and answers arising from that occasion have justifiably faded into the mists of history, of interest only to students of presidential trivia. But one item has not been forgotten, and with good reason. When Rupert Richards of Copley Press asked Eisenhower to assess the value of Indochina for the United States and its allies, the president responded that Southeast Asia was an area of great significance and concern for the Western powers. He elaborated on this, saying, "You have a row of dominos set up, you knock over the first one, and what will happen to the last one is the certainty that it will go over very quickly. So you could have a beginning of a disintegration that would have the most profound influences."[1]

This was the first public articulation of what has become known as the "domino theory." As this chapter will reveal, it was not to be the last. In the discussion that follows, I will show the importance of the domino theory to both presidential decision making about involvement in Vietnam and the rhetoric used to justify and secure support for those decisions. I will also examine the use of the domino theory as a condensation symbol by U.S. presidents from Harry Truman to Richard Nixon, along with the implications of such usage.

THE IMPORTANCE OF THE DOMINO THEORY

It would be a foolish exaggeration to suggest that the domino theory was the sole premise on which American decisions about Southeast Asia were based in the years following World War II. The pervasive importance of the "falling dominos" concept is difficult to overestimate, however. The domino theory, with its assumption that the fall of one Third World country to Communism would inevitably lead to the subversion, in sequence, of neighboring countries, was a basic tenet of many American leaders throughout the Cold War.[2] During the Eisenhower and Kennedy years, the domino principle was, in the worlds of James S. Olson and Randy Roberts, "central to the way Americans interpreted the world, rivaling the Monroe Doctrine and the Open Door in importance."[3] Nor did belief in the theory fade as the Cold War widened; the image of dominos in descent had staying power. Indeed, the theory was perhaps the most resilient of the various notions used to describe international relations in the Cold War era.[4] As Jay Shafritz described it, the domino principle was "a major element in the rationale for American involvement in the Vietnam War."[5]

But the domino theory was more than an idea to be bandied about in the hushed conference rooms of Washington, D.C. It was employed rhetorically by several administrations to generate support for U.S. policies in Southeast Asia. In 1954, the Eisenhower administration was using the domino theory in an effort to secure cooperation from the British and French for joint action with the United States to prevent a Viet Minh victory in North Vietnam.[6] The allies were unpersuaded, however, and no cooperative action was taken. Shortly thereafter, the fall of Dien Bien Phu seemed to show that the United States would undertake any future action largely alone. From that point, the rhetorical use of the domino theory was focused mainly on the American public. If unilateral U.S. action were to be required, then public opinion would have to be brought around to endorse it. The rhetoric dedicated to this was effective for quite a long time. As Loren Baritz concluded, through the use of the domino theory, "a peripheral problem was redefined as the flaming fuse on an explosive that could obliterate freedom in the world. This was a concept the American public could understand and support."[7]

Rhetoric based on the domino theory became especially effective for the Eisenhower administration once Senator Joseph McCarthy initiated the anti-Communist hysteria that would later bear his name. Some of the widespread fear of Communism at home could be channeled into concern about Communist advances abroad; thus, the notion of underdeveloped countries succumbing to Communism, like dominos pushed over by a large (Red) finger, caught on and was widely accepted.[8]

The rhetorical utility of the domino theory did not end with Mc-Carthyism, however. It would serve other presidents after Eisenhower for reasons that F. M. Kail clearly delineates:

As a rhetorical device, the domino principle was a dramatic way of demonstrating that an apparently peripheral contest could, strategically, be of pivotal significance. An all or nothing proposition—either the first domino was saved or all were doomed—it had the virtue of being both simple and graphic. . . . The domino principle was not at bottom an attempt to explain or to offer a theory of international dynamics; it was, rather, more an effort to rally support for a potentially dangerous foreign adventure.[9]

A major reason for the domino theory's success as a rhetorical proposition was its use as a condensation symbol by several administrations. The nature and import of condensation symbols are discussed below.

CONDENSATION SYMBOLS IN POLITICAL RHETORIC

When used verbally, a condensation symbol is "a name, word phrase, or maxim which stirs vivid impressions involving the listener's most basic values."[10] In political rhetoric, a condensation symbol is often general enough to have meaning across a wide spectrum of audience members but also sufficiently specific to provoke the emotional response desired by the rhetor using it. In the 1980s, Ronald Reagan demonstrated his understanding of condensation symbols when he attempted to create significant public support for his policies toward Nicaragua. In Reagan's public discourse, those Nicaraguans in exile who were attempting to overthrow by force the Marxist government of Manuel Ortega were never "contras" as they were usually called in the news media but always "Nicaraguan freedom fighters." In at least one instance, Reagan described these insurgents, some of whom were former members of Nicaraguan dictator Anastasio Somoza's secret police and were alleged to be involved in the international cocaine traffic, as "the moral equivalent of the Founding Fathers."[11] Those Americans who accepted the president's analogy may not have had in mind any specific points of comparison between the Nicaraguan counterrevolutionaries and such persons as Thomas Jefferson and Alexander Hamilton, but they knew the Founding Fathers were good men who struggled for justice. For some Americans who came to support Reagan's Nicaraguan policies, this was enough.

Clearly, condensation symbols are more than neutral descriptors. In Murray Edelman's words, they "evoke the emotions associated with the situation."[12] In doing so, condensation symbols discourage objective analysis of the concept described; "the constant check of the immediate environment is lacking."[13]

The use of condensation symbols benefits the political rhetor in a number of ways. For one, it allows the speaker to express a fairly complex idea succinctly. The terms "Star Wars" and "SDI" (Strategic Defense Initiative) thus came to stand for an intricate, technologically advanced space-based missile defense system. Indeed, these two references often appeared on opposite sides of the controversy over the system's deployment that raged during the Reagan years. The administration and others supporting the program usually referred to it with the relatively formal, technocratic sounding "SDI." Opponents, many of whom believed that the proper place for such an idea was in a science fiction movie, preferred the slightly derisive "Star Wars."

A second advantage of the political use of condensation symbols is that it allows a leader, whether in government or a social movement, to build consensus. Since condensation symbols tend to have both broad and deep meanings that are vague enough to gain wide acceptance and evocative enough to invoke strong feelings, they are well suited for rhetoric aimed at a mass audience. This was demonstrated in the 1988 presidential election. The Bush campaign effectively employed the American flag as a condensation symbol to build Bush's support and undermine that of Michael Dukakis. While governor of Massachusetts years earlier, Dukakis had killed a proposed state law mandating that the Pledge of Allegiance be recited daily in all the commonwealth's public schools. Bush strategists claimed that this decision, which Dukakis had made on expert advice that the law would be unconstitutional, showed that Dukakis was against the Pledge of Allegiance and hence, against the American flag. This accusation was implicit rather than explicit, but the message was clear to many. Bush began to give campaign speeches at flag factories, references to the flag and the Pledge became prominent in his rhetoric, and the number and size of American flags at his campaign stops increased dramatically. Dukakis fought back with massive flag displays of his own, but the damage had been done. Many voters had decided that if Dukakis were against the Pledge of Allegiance, he must also be against the flag, and that if he failed to love the American flag, he could not really love America.

A third value of condensation symbols stems from their giving a political leader the ability to define the terms under which discussion will take place. The names given to things determine how those so named will be perceived. As Hugh Duncan observed, political ideas "are *names*, and whoever creates or controls those names controls our lives."[14] During the civil rights movement of the 1950s and 1960s when many white Southerners were persuaded by their leaders to blame much of the local demand for racial equality as the work of "outside agitators," those leaders were well on the way to shifting responsibility from local injustices to imported troublemakers. A few decades earlier, Adolf Hitler and other Nazi leaders referred to Jews as "untermenschen" (subhumans). With this and other linguistic devices employed in their public discourse, the Nazis were laying the groundwork for a program with another "special" name: "resettlement," also known less widely as "the Final Solution."

While condensation symbols have their uses for political leaders, they pose potential dangers for the body politic. Some of those dangers have been implied by the examples used above, but a more detailed discussion seems called for.

The use of condensation symbols in political discourse involves at least two major dangers. The first is oversimplification. By definition, condensation symbols require simple, if emotionally charged, ideas. But not all political ideas are simple, nor should they be. John F. Kennedy's 1960 campaign pledge to "get the country moving again" had a pleasant sound to it, but it conveyed little information about his plans for the nation's invigoration. George Bush's notion of a "new world order" fell on appreciative ears immediately following the successful conclusion of Operation Desert Storm, but Mr. Bush, as of this writing, has yet to delineate the specific components of this international arrangement or the reasons why Americans should welcome them.

A second danger arising from the political use of condensation symbols is that a clever leader can cause them to be widely accepted by the public without question, discussion, or debate. This not only subverts the right of free speech that democracies value, but also often leads to silly ideas or even malicious falsehoods achieving the status of Holy Writ. Senator Joseph McCarthy warned America in the 1950s of a "domestic Communist conspiracy" that threatened to defeat the nation from within. The spirit of the times, combined with McCarthy's talent for demogoguery, caused this notion, since proven to be utterly untrue, to acquire an aura of fundamental validity. Indeed, anyone in public life who questioned the existence of the domestic Communist conspiracy ran the risk of being lumped with those taking part in that alleged cabal.[15]

Condensation symbols also played their role in the discourse concerning American involvement in the Vietnam War. Cal Logue and John Patton have demonstrated how Lyndon Johnson used the symbols of "peacemaker," "enemy," and "savior" to persuade Americans to support his escalation of U.S. bombing and troop commitments.[16] Kennedy's support for "counterinsurgency" probably caused the term to serve as a condensation symbol, at least for policymakers, and this gave rise to the goal of "winning hearts and minds," which was another. Richard Nixon added at least two: the "silent majority" and "peace with honor." But no condensation symbol of the Vietnam era saw more presidential usage in the long term, or achieved greater rhetorical and political importance, than the domino theory.

THE DOMINO THEORY IN PRESIDENTIAL RHETORIC

Robert Donovan wrote that "[t]he domino theory, under one name or another, became an article of faith among American presidents" in the postwar era.[17] As we will see, the concept occupied a prominent place in much presidential rhetoric, as well.

President Harry Truman never referred to the domino theory by that name, but the idea had its roots in his administration and his discourse. The Truman Doctrine, articulated in an April 1947 address, was the domino theory applied to the Mediterranean. Truman was asking Congress for significant foreign aid to Greece and Turkey, and he warned of dire consequences for the whole region if those two nations should fall to Communist subversion:

If Greece should fall under the control of an armed minority, the effect upon its neighbor, Turkey, would be immediate and serious. Confusion and disorder might well spread throughout the entire Middle East.

Moreover, the disappearance of Greece as an independent state would have a profound effect upon those countries in Europe whose peoples are struggling against great difficulties to maintain their freedoms and their independence while they repair the damages of war.[18]

A few years later, the scene had shifted to Asia, but the argument was essentially the same. In his effort to beef up support for U.S. involvement in the Korean conflict, Truman told members of Congress, "If we let Korea down the Soviets will keep right on going and swallow up one piece of Asia after another. . . . If we were to let Asia go, the Near East would collapse and no telling what would happen in Europe."[19]

In this, Truman was articulating what he had been hearing from his National Security Council (NSC) for some time. An NSC memorandum in February 1950 held that "[t]he neighboring countries of Thailand and Burma could be expected to fall under Communist domination if Indochina is controlled by a Communist government. The balance of Southeast Asia would then be in grave hazard."[20] Two years later, the NSC was playing the same tune, but with additional lyrics:

[T]he loss of any single country [in Southeast Asia] would probably lead to relatively swift submission to or an alignment with Communism by the remaining countries of this group. Furthermore, an alignment with Communism of the rest of Southeast Asia and India, and in the longer term, of the Middle East . . . would in all probability progressively follow: Such widespread alignment would endanger the stability and security of Europe.[21]

Thus, it seems evident that the domino theory was not only a mechanism of presidential persuasion directed at the public but also a means by which some presidents were themselves influenced. Considering the assessments that Truman was receiving from the National Security Council, along with the rhetoric he was moved to create in response to that information, one should not be surprised to learn that "[m]uch of what would become known as the 'domino theory' was in place when the Truman administration left office."[22]

Eisenhower's first public use of the image of falling dominos to represent the status of Southeast Asia has already been mentioned. But he was advocating the idea in other terms and for other places as early as 1951. In February of that year, citizen Eisenhower told a NATO gathering that the fall of free Europe to Communism would mean that "many economically dependent areas in Africa and the Middle East would be affected by this debacle. Southeast Asia would probably soon be lost."[23] Three years later, as we have seen, a shift took place. Instead of being portrayed as the last domino in a series beginning in Western Europe, Indochina was seen as the first, and, hence, most vulnerable, in a row that extended *back* to Europe.

There were two reasons for this change of focus from West to East. One was the Korean War, which showed the power of aggressive Communism in Asia and how difficult it was to stop. The hole in freedom's dike had been plugged after years of fighting, but Eisenhower was convinced that the next leak was ready to spurt in Vietnam.[24]

The second reason was the "loss" of China and its effect on the American political scene. The success of Mao's revolution had led to an orgy of recriminations from America's political right.[25] This had caused considerable difficulty for Truman, although he had done nothing to cause or permit the Communist victory, and had left the country ripe for McCarthy's Red-baiting demagoguery. Eisenhower was conscious of the continuous pressure emanating from the most conservative elements of his own party, and their message was clear: no more Asian countries must succumb to Communism.[26]

Thus did Eisenhower come to see Indochina as the "first domino" and to portray it as such in his rhetoric. After the 1954 press conference in which the falling domino principle was first advanced, the president and his spokesman returned to this theme time and again in their public talk.[27] This continued with little pause for reflection until May, when the fall of the garrison at Dien Bien Phu spelled the end of French hegemony in Vietnam. Two months later, the Geneva Accords divided Vietnam into two nations, with the Communists firmly in control of the north.

This turn of events caused some in the Eisenhower administration to think aloud about the domino theory. Did the Communist victory in North Vietnam mean that the first piece had already fallen, with the rest of Asia to follow? Or was the domino principle to be abandoned, lest U.S. allies in the region lose hope? The answer to this conundrum was found by Secretary of State John Foster Dulles, who was in many ways Eisenhower's main Cold War strategist. The theory was still valid, Dulles insisted. But North Vietnam was not the first element in the chain. Rather, the crucial domino was in the South. If the Saigon government succumbed to Communist subversion, only *then* would the rest of the region be in peril. "Like a true believer whose strength of conviction only increases when prophecy fails, [Dulles] still believed in the domino theory."[28]

Eisenhower's continued support of the falling domino principle was buttressed by both his secretary of state and his National Security Council. The president had been told in January 1954 (three months before his press conference reference to falling dominos) that the "loss of any single country" in Indochina would lead to the collapse of the entire region.[29] In August, he convened another NSC meeting to consider current policies toward Southeast Asia. Support for the domino theory was unanimous among those attending.[30]

Thus, the domino theory not only gained its name, along with the rhetorical power of a metaphor, during Eisenhower's term—but also attracted many fervent adherents. Eisenhower was persuaded to endorse the concept by both political necessity and the views of his most trusted advisers. In his last months in office, he did his best to pass on his convictions about the domino theory to the young senator from Massachusetts who was about to succeed him.[31]

When Eisenhower spoke to John Kennedy about the importance of the domino theory, he was likely preaching to the converted. As far back as 1956, Kennedy was advocating the concept, albeit without the "domino" metaphor. In a well-publicized speech, the junior senator from Massachusetts described South Vietnam as

the cornerstone of the free world in Southeast Asia, the keystone to the arch, the finger in the dike. Burma, Thailand, Indonesia, Japan, the Philippines, and obviously Laos and Cambodia are among those whose security would be threatened if the red tide of Communism overflowed into Vietnam.[32]

Some say that Kennedy, as president, found the domino theory unpersuasive. William Safire quotes political writer Arthur Krock, who claimed, after an interview with Kennedy, that "[t]he President expressed doubts that [the domino] theory had much point any more." Krock alleged that Kennedy told him that Communist China would eventually develop a nuclear capability and thereafter would dominate much of Asia, U.S. efforts notwithstanding.[33]

But other evidence suggests that Kennedy was an adherent of the domino theory—and no evidence is better than his own words. In an interview with television's "Huntley-Brinkley Report" in September 1963, the president was asked whether he had reservations concerning the domino theory. He replied:

No, I believe it. I believe it. I think that the struggle is close enough. China is so large, looms so high just beyond the frontiers, that if South Vietnam went, it would not only give them an improved geographic position for a guerrilla assault on Malaya, but it would also give the impression that the wave of the future in southeast Asia was China and the Communists. So I believe it.[34]

Walt Rostow, who had been one of Kennedy's closest advisers on the Vietnam issue, later characterized this interview as Kennedy's "flattest reaffirmation . . . of the domino theory."[35]

If Kennedy's belief in the theory remained unshaken, it was partly because his advisers looked to Asia and saw a row of dominos themselves. All the members of the president's inner circle of foreign policy experts backed the domino theory unhesitatingly. "There was," in Jaya Krisha Baral's words, "no conflict on the perspective."[36] In January 1962, the Joint Chiefs of Staff sent Kennedy a memorandum concluding that the "loss" of Southeast Asia would have dramatic and tragic results for U.S. influence throughout the Third World.[37] The dominos, in other words, would tumble if pushed.

Within the administration, the domino theory had no more dedicated advocate than Defense Secretary Robert McNamara. McNamara espoused the concept from his earliest days at the Pentagon's helm, and he championed it at Congressional hearings for a long time thereafter. "Year after year, [McNamara] repeated the pattern of waving the 'domino' theory as the basis of the American policy in Vietnam."[38]

Such was the persuasiveness of the Kennedy administration's rhetoric that even the *New York Times*, hardly a bastion of conservative sabre rattling, appeared to echo Kennedy's "Huntley-Brinkley" answer less than two months after he gave it:

the loss of South Vietnam to the Communists could raise doubts around the globe about the value of U.S. commitments to defend nations against Communist pressure. . . . The impact on revolutionary movements throughout the world would be profound. At best, neutralism in the East-West struggle might spread. In much of Asia there might be a feeling that the Communists—under the leadership and inspiration of Peking—represented "the wave of the future."[39]

Clearly, the credibility of the domino theory and its implications for U.S. policy went essentially unchanged from Eisenhower's administration to Kennedy's.[40] Despite the differences in style (rhetorically and otherwise) between the two presidents, the message was essentially the same. Kennedy was convinced that the "long twilight struggle" would have to be carried out in Vietnam, although he was determined to keep American troop involvement limited—primarily to the U.S. Army's Special Forces. Whether Kennedy's goal of limited American military presence could have been maintained in later years is not known. On November 22, 1963, the problem passed from Kennedy's hands to those of Lyndon Johnson.

Johnson, like Kennedy, had expressed support for the domino theory before taking office. Kennedy had sent his vice president to Vietnam on an inspection tour in 1961, and Johnson's report on returning contained a strong endorsement of the falling dominos principle. He wrote: "[t]he battle against communism must be joined in Southeast Asia with strength and determination to achieve success there—or the United States, inevitably, must surrender the Pacific and take up our defenses on our own shores."[41]

As president, Johnson continued to support the domino theory in his rhetoric. In a June 2, 1964, news conference, for example, he outlined "four basic themes that govern our policy in Southeast Asia," one of which was "the issue of Southeast Asia as a whole."[42] In other words, Johnson was arguing that the defense of South Vietnam was the key to the future of the entire region—which is the essence of the domino theory, pure and simple.[43]

As was the case with Kennedy and his two predecessors, Johnson received little contradiction of the falling dominos principle from his advisers. Indeed, one experienced Washington journalist was quoted in a 1969 *Newsweek* article as saying that, during the Johnson years, "everybody and his grandmother used the domino analogy in one fashion or another, although it was always more of a state of mind than an articulated policy."[44]

But, as we have seen, at times it *was* an articulated policy. When Johnson was not speaking of it publicly, his surrogates often were. In 1964, for example, rhetoric in support of the falling domino principle was often forthcoming from those close to the president. Secretary of State Dean Rusk claimed that a U.S. surrender in Vietnam "would mean . . . grevious [sic] losses to the free world in Southeast Asia and Southern Asia."[45] The U.S. ambassador to South Vietnam, Henry Cabot Lodge, maintained that "the well-advertised domino theory applies here,"[46] and General Maxwell Taylor predicted that "[a]fter Communist success in South Vietnam, the remainder of Southeast Asia would very shortly thereafter go neutralist, possibly eventually Communist."[47] During a visit to Japan, Assistant Secretary of State William P. Bundy warned that, if the Communists should win in Vietnam, "the rest of Southeast Asia will be in grave danger of progressively disappearing behind the Bamboo Curtain and other Asian countries like India and even in time Australia" would be ripe for conquest or subversion.[48]

In private, Johnson's men tended to be as adamant as they were in their public talk. In a June 1965 cabinet meeting, Secretary of State Rusk strongly backed the falling dominos idea.[49] A month later, at a meeting with Johnson and the Joint Chiefs of Staff, Defense Secretary McNamara took the domino theory to a level that almost qualifies as a *reductio ad absurdum*: if South Vietnam fell, he argued, the impact would ultimately affect not only Southeast Asia but also Japan, India, Pakistan, Greece, Turkey, even Africa.[50]

Amidst all of this geographical gloom and doom, a ray of sunshine and sanity appeared from an unlikely source: the Central Intelligence Agency (CIA). Johnson knew that his plans for increased troop deployments in Vietnam would require public support and that skillful rhetoric would thus be required. He therefore asked the CIA for a report estimating the probable effects that a Communist victory in Vietnam would have on the rest of Asia. The president assumed the report would give him additional evidence to use in his campaign to sell the new troop commitments to the American people. His assumption proved incorrect.

The CIA document was a blunt refutation of the domino theory as Johnson and his advisers had been interpreting it for several years. It read, in part:

With the possible exception of Cambodia, it is likely that no nation in the area would quickly succumb to Communism as a result of the fall of Laos and South Vietnam. Furthermore, a continuation of the spread of Communism in the area would not be inexorable, and any spread which did occur would take time— time in which the total situation might change in any number of ways unfavorable to the Communist cause.[51]

The president and his advisers rejected the CIA's analysis, and the Agency's role in Vietnam decision making was sharply reduced thereafter. As Baritz wrote, the report "challenged basic elements in the developing American theology about Vietnam [and thus] ran the risk of being ignored by the war's clergymen."[52] That is what the domino theory had become by 1964: an article of faith, a doctrine to be believed and preached to the unconverted—not a hypothesis to be viewed critically and tested. Perhaps that is what the domino theory had always been.

The Tet Offensive of 1968 effectively ended Lyndon Johnson's pursuit of the Holy Grail of victory in Vietnam. His successor, Richard Nixon, had his own agenda for the struggle in Vietnam and his own views on the domino theory.

Nixon never hoped to "win" the Vietnam War. From the start of his administration, the goals were to withdraw American forces, turn the fighting over to the South Vietnamese, and achieve a negotiated settlement with Hanoi. All of this had to be done, however, in such a way to avoid the impression that Nixon had led the nation to defeat in Vietnam. This idea would be encapsulated in the slogan "Peace with Honor," which Nixon would repeat time and again.

Nixon recognized the need to employ rhetoric to justify the slow pace of American disengagement, as well as occasional aggressive actions such as the incursion into Cambodia and the mining of Haiphong Harbor. Thus was the domino theory trotted out again, like a tired old warhorse rescued from the glue factory at the last minute. Nixon did not really place much faith in the concept of falling dominos; neither did Henry Kissinger, the national security adviser who would later become secretary of state. But both men were willing to use it to buy time.[53]

Thus, Nixon told reporters in 1970, "I know there are those who say the domino theory is obsolete. They haven't talked to the dominoes."[54] For his part, Kissinger maintained that "[t]he stability of areas geographically far removed from Vietnam will be basically affected by the outcome there." He claimed that, in Vietnam, Americans were "fighting for ourselves and international stability."[55] These and other examples of administration rhetoric led *Newsweek* to conclude that "[d]ominoes, it seems, is still the name of the game in Washington."[56] As history has shown, this was far from the truth. The name of the game was "Peace with Honor," and the domino theory was only a gambit within the overall strategy, to be used when necessary and then forgotten.

Kissinger declared that "peace is at hand," somewhat prematurely, in the fall of 1972, and the last American combat troops were out of Vietnam by the spring of the following year. Saigon fell to the North Vietnamese in April 1975. As the Communists were rolling up the South Vietnamese army like a moth-eaten rug, U.S. political leaders were busy assuring their people that the domino theory had never really been a valid concept, after all. The Third World was not about to suffer inevitable Communist subversion, U.S. influence was not on the wane throughout the globe, and the dawning of a new era of peace could bring only good things to a nation that had struggled so valiantly in the cause of freedom.[57]

In a televised address to Congress on April 10, 1975, President Gerald Ford told the nation that "the spirit of America is good and the heart of America is strong. Let us be proud of what we have done and confident of what we can do."[58] Although he did discuss the rapidly deteriorating situation in Vietnam, Ford also reminded his audience of America's many foreign policy successes since the end of World War II—not a few of which involved countries that had been characterized as "dominos" by prior administrations. The *Washington Post* responded to this message with approval, noting: "President Ford quietly banished the domino theory from presidential policy."[59]

Two weeks later, in a speech at Tulane University, the president continued with this theme, saying, "We, of course, are saddened indeed by the events in Indochina. But these events, tragic as they are, portend neither the end of the world nor of America's leadership in the world."[60]

There were those who believed that the domino theory died that spring, like a vampire exposed to sunlight at last. As a series of "Dracula" movies produced by Hammer Films in the 1960s demonstrated, however, sometimes even dead vampires can come back to life.

Five years after the fall of South Vietnam, Ronald Reagan revived the domino theory, while rejecting the lessons of the Vietnam War.[61] Shortly before taking office, Reagan gave an interview in which he blamed the Soviet Union for most of the world's troubles. Soviet subversion, he argued, "underlies all the unrest that is going on. If they weren't engaged in this game of dominoes, there wouldn't be any hot spots in the world."[62] Reagan would later apply the concept of descending dominos to justify his policies toward El Salvador and Nicaragua.[63] Such policies, and such rhetoric, were responsible for the appearance in the 1980s of anti-intervention bumper stickers that read, "El Salvador is Spanish for Vietnam."

IMPLICATIONS OF THE USE OF THE DOMINO THEORY

This last section considers the economic, cultural, and political aspects that were all part, albeit implicitly, of the domino theory. Some of these involve assumptions that underlay the concept, and others consist of effects stemming from the domino theory's application.

Much of the anxiety about chain reaction Communist subversion that drove the domino theory was, in Richard Barnet's words, "a profound fear of economic loss."[64] The presumption of loss stemmed from the idea that the raw materials of a given region would be denied to the West if the Communists should gain control there. In the press conference in which the domino theory received its name, for example, Eisenhower referred to the resources of tin, rubber, and tungsten that would become unavailable if the dominos began to tumble in Asia. Marilyn Young may have put it best: "Vietnam was a domino whose 'fall' would turn the Pacific into a Soviet lake, denying vital raw materials to the United States and its allies."[65]

The ethical and moral dimensions of this economic outlook were never examined publicly (or, perhaps, even privately) by U.S. leaders. Whether the United States had a right to the Third World's natural resources was a question not raised in presidential rhetoric, nor was the question of whether U.S. support for any and all anti-Communist governments in developing countries was anything more than an excuse for economic exploitation.[66]

The domino theory may also have been based on assumptions that

were culturally chauvinistic, if not patently racist. When groups of nations are reduced to black and white game pieces for purpose of analysis
and discussion, they lose all individuality. Consideration of a country's
culture, history, and government becomes irrelevant. All developing
countries are presumed to be identical, and if one in the row is knocked
over, then the others will inevitably follow; dominos are not allowed to
argue with the laws of physics or gravity. Some scholars tried to remind
Lyndon Johnson is 1965 that "despite elements of similarity, no Southeast Asian nation is a replica of any other."[67] There is no evidence that
Johnson heeded this information. Indeed, the record supports the conclusion reached by T. D. Allman, that "[t]he domino theory flows from
the doctrine of American superiority; since there 'is no alternative to
United States leadership,' even those who do accept our leadership are
inherently inferior."[68] In short, as James Thomson argued, the domino
theory "resulted from profound ignorance of Asian history and hence
ignorance of the radical differences among Asian nations and
societies."[69]

One effect of the use of the domino theory was to give Vietnam a
degree of importance (in terms of U.S. interests) that it did not, objectively, deserve. Asia was clearly a relevant area of concern for U.S.
policymakers, but Indochina was not the key to Asian stability—except
that Communist success in North Vietnam made it appear so. "Indochina was of little intrinsic importance or interest [to the United States].
But as perceived lynchpin in the crescent that stretched between India
and Japan, it was seen as vital."[70] The presence of Ho Chi Minh's Communist government in the North made South Vietnam the crucial domino, the "weakest link" in a chain that might stretch to Japan, Australia,
or even Hawaii, depending on one's perception of the domino theory.[71]
Since the doctrine held that the fall of one element would inevitably
send the others tumbling, the country seen as most likely to succumb
automatically assumed gigantic significance, quite apart from its actual
geopolitical importance. Therefore, because of the perceptions growing
out of belief in the domino theory, a country of rice paddies and water
buffalo became the testing ground for American power—with tragic
consequences for all concerned.

Another effect stemming from the rhetorical use of the domino theory
was that it provided added credibility for the Johnson administration's
"aggression thesis" concerning Vietnam. Prior to Johnson's escalation
of the war in early 1965, the administration's position had been that the
turmoil in Vietnam was caused by indigenous Communist insurgents.
After stepping up the bombing and troop commitments, however, Johnson and his men began arguing that the Vietnamese situation was one
of external aggression by a hostile foreign government—that is, Hanoi.[72]

Although Johnson's rhetoric did not explicitly link the domino theory with the aggression thesis, the former surely facilitated Americans' belief in the latter. A row of dominos, after all, does not knock itself over; it requires a push from something other than the dominos, something outside. Thus, belief in the domino theory made it easy to perceive the Vietnamese Communists as "an alien hegemonic movement."[73] As James William Gibson put it, in the worldview created by the domino theory,

[t]he foreign Other, Communist antinature, invades and destroys the natural order of Vietnam (capitalism). If Vietnam "falls" to Communism, then the rest of Asia will surely follow . . . an inevitable, inexorable mechanical process. . . . Within the logic of the domino theory, all of South Vietnam's problems came from beyond, the place where the foreign Other lived.[74]

Thus, with the Communists successfully labeled as "foreign Other," it was easy for Johnson to support the charge of external aggression. Further, defending a nation against outside aggression is a much more persuasive justification than intervening in another country's civil war.

Perhaps the ultimate irony of the domino theory is that it was no theory at all. In another sense, it was more than a theory. A theory, after all, is basically a working hypothesis to be subjected to empirical examination. The domino theory was never subjected to critical scrutiny by any U.S. president from Truman to Johnson (and perhaps not since, either). As the *Pentagon Papers* revealed, "The domino theory and the assumptions behind it were never questioned."[75] It was more a mindset than a theory; it was a way of looking at the world that was stubbornly resistant to change. Given its influence on twenty-five years of U.S. policy toward Southeast Asia, it may be prudent to agree with Walter LaFeber, who wrote, "The domino theory was (and remains) one of the most dangerous of ideas that attract Americans."[76]

NOTES

1. Dwight D. Eisenhower, "The President's News Conference of April 7, 1954," in *Public Papers of the Presidents of the United States: Dwight D. Eisenhower, 1954* (Washington, DC: Government Printing Office, 1958), 73. This source will hereafter be referred to as *PPP*.

2. Larry Berman, *Planning A Tragedy* (New York: W. W. Norton, 1982), 130.

3. James S. Olson and Randy Roberts, *Where the Domino Fell* (New York: St. Martin's Press, 1991), 29.

4. Gabriel Kolko, *Anatomy of a War* (New York: Pantheon Books, 1985), 74.

5. Jay M. Shafritz, *The Dorsey Dictionary of American Government and Politics* (Chicago: The Dorsey Press, 1988), 175.

6. F. M. Kail, *What Washington Said* (New York: Harper & Row, 1973), 87.

7. Loren Baritz, *Backfire* (New York: William Morrow, 1985), 80.

8. Olson and Roberts, 30.

9. Kail, 88–89.

10. Doris A. Graber, *Verbal Behavior and Politics* (Urbana, IL: University of Illinois Press, 1976), 289.

11. Ronald Reagan, "Remarks at the Annual Dinner of the Conservative Political Action Conference, March 1, 1985," in *PPP: Ronald Reagan, 1985* 1 (Washington, DC: Government Printing Office, 1988), 229.

12. Murray Feldman, *The Symbolic Uses of Politics* (Urbana, IL: University of Illinois Press, 1967), 6.

13. Ibid.

14. Hugh Dalziel Duncan, *Symbols in Society* (London: Oxford University Press, 1968), 33.

15. This discussion of the uses and dangers of condensation symbols is adapted from Graber, 289–311.

16. Cal M. Logue and John H. Patton, "From Ambiguity to Dogma: The Rhetorical Symbols of Lyndon B. Johnson on Vietnam," *The Southern Speech Communication Journal* 47 (1982): 315–21.

17. Robert T. Donovan, *Nemesis* (New York: St. Martin's Press, 1984), 22.

18. Harry S. Truman, "Special Message to the Congress on Greece and Turkey: The Truman Doctrine, March 12, 1947," *PPP: Harry S. Truman, 1947* (Washington, DC: Government Printing Office, 1963), 179.

19. Quoted in Baritz, 69.

20. *The Pentagon Papers* (New York: Quadrangle Books, 1971), 7.

21. Ibid., 28.

22. James R. Arnold, *The First Domino* (New York: William Morrow, 1991), 83–84.

23. Quoted in J. Fred MacDonald, *Television and the Red Menace* (New York: Praeger, 1985), 64.

24. Marilyn B. Young, *The Vietnam Wars: 1945–1990* (New York: Harper Collins, 1991), 30.

25. Donovan, 22.

26. William H. Chafe, *The Unfinished Journey* (New York: Oxford University Press, 1986), 258.

27. Kail, 86.

28. Arnold, 234.

29. Quoted in *The Pentagon Papers*, 8.

30. Berman, 11.

31. Arnold, 377.

32. John F. Kennedy, "America's Stake in Vietnam," *Vital Speeches of the Day* 22 (1956): 619.

33. William Safire, *Safire's Political Dictionary* (New York: Random House, 1978), 179.

34. John F. Kennedy, "Transcript of Broadcast on NBC's Huntley-Brinkley Report, September 9, 1963," *PPP: John F. Kennedy, 1963* (Washington, DC: Government Printing Office, 1964), 659.

35. Quoted in Henry Lamont, "Rostow Likens War Policies of Presidents Kennedy and Johnson," *The New York Times*, April 21, 1969, 16.

36. Jaya Krishna Baral, *The Pentagon and the Making of U.S. Foreign Policy* (Atlantic Highlands, NJ: Humanities Press, 1978), 178.

37. *The Pentagon Papers*, 158–159.

38. Baral, 254.

39. Quoted in Earl C. Ravenal, "Consequences of the End Game in Vietnam," *Foreign Affairs* 53 (1975): 653.

40. Baritz, 129.

41. Quoted in Donovan, 43.

42. Lyndon B. Johnson, "The President's News Conference of June 2, 1964," *PPP: Lyndon B. Johnson, 1963–64* 1 (Washington, DC: Government Printing Office, 1965), 733.

43. MacDonald, 208.

44. "The Falling Dominos," *Newsweek*, October 27, 1969, 24.

45. Quoted in Kail, 90.

46. Ibid., 91.

47. Ibid.

48. Ibid.

49. VanDeMark, 166.

50. Ibid., 196.

51. Quoted in *The Pentagon Papers*, 262.

52. Baritz, 139.

53. Ibid., 195.

54. Richard Nixon, "A Conversation with the President about Foreign Policy, July 1, 1970," *PPP: Richard Nixon, 1970* (Washington, DC: Government Printing Office, 1971), 546–547.

55. "The Falling Dominos," 24.

56. Ibid.

57. Levy, 173.

58. Gerald R. Ford, "Address before a Joint Session of Congress Reporting on United States Foreign Policy, April 10, 1975," *PPP: Gerald R. Ford, 1975* 1 (Washington, DC: Government Printing Office, 1977), 570.

59. Quoted in Ravenal, 653.

60. Gerald R. Ford, "Address at a Tulane University Convocation, April 23, 1975," *PPP: Gerald R. Ford, 1975* 1 (Washington, DC: Government Printing Office, 1977), 570.

61. Thomas G. Patterson, *Meeting the Communist Threat: Truman to Reagan* (New York: Oxford University Press, 1988), 256.

62. Quoted in Hedrick Smith, "Reagan: What Kind of World Leader?" *The New York Times Magazine*, November 16, 1980, 172.

63. Edward P. Morgan, *The 60s Experience* (Philadelphia, PA: Temple University Press, 1991), 254.

64. Richard J. Barnet, *Roots of War* (New York: Penguin Books, 1972), 160.

65. Young, 29.

66. Kolko, 77.

67. Quoted in William Appleman Williams, Thomas McCormick, Lloyd Gardner, and Walter LaFeber, eds., *America in Vietnam: A Documentary History* (Garden City, NY: Anchor Books, 1985), 231.

68. T. D. Allman, *Unmanifest Destiny* (Garden City, NY: The Dial Press, 1984), 292.

69. James C. Thomson, Jr., "How Could Vietnam Happen? An Autopsy," in *The American Experience in Vietnam: A Reader*, ed. Grace Sevy (Norman, OK: University of Oklahoma Press, 1989), 38.

70. Thomas McCormick, "Crisis, Commitment, and Counter-revolution, 1945–1952," in Sevy, 23.

71. Kolko, 77.

72. F. Michael Smith, "Rhetorical Implications of the 'Aggression' Thesis in the Johnson Administration's Vietnam Argumentation," *Central States Speech Journal* 23 (1972): 218.

73. Jerry Mark Silverman, "The Domino Theory: Alternatives to a Self-Fulfilling Prophecy," *Asian Survey* 15 (1975): 916.

74. James William Gibson, *The Perfect War* (Boston: Atlantic Monthly Press, 1986), 26, 226.

75. *The Pentagon Papers*, 8.

76. Williams et al., 231.

Chapter Two

John F. Kennedy and the Green Berets: The Rhetorical Use of the Hero Myth

Scholars have long been aware of the importance of myth to the rhetoric of politics and government. As Lance Bennett has argued, "Myths condition the public to the powerful symbols used by politicians."[1] Some studies in this area have focused abroad, examining the role of myth in the rhetoric of such figures as Fidel Castro[2] and Adolf Hitler.[3] Others have concentrated on the American scene and have discussed the political use of myth in such different rhetorical contexts as the American Revolution,[4] imperialism by the United States and Great Britain,[5] antiwar rhetoric,[6] the rhetorical impact of China's fall to Communism on U.S. politics,[7] Daniel Webster's oratory,[8] the opposition to the Equal Rights Amendment,[9] presidential campaigns,[10] the genre of presidential inaugural addresses,[11] and specific presidential speeches.[12]

One political figure whose rhetorical use of myth has been largely neglected is President John F. Kennedy. Although Janice Hocker Rushing examined Kennedy's use of the myth to invigorate the U.S. space program,[13] the mythic aspects of this president's rhetoric have not been a popular focus for scholars.

One unexamined aspect of Kennedy's mythic rhetoric seems particularly deserving of attention: his use of the U.S. Army Special Forces as manifestations of the powerful hero myth. In a recent study of American myth and the Vietnam War, John Hellman wrote:

John F. Kennedy had energized Americans with his vision of their heroic possibilities on a New Frontier. He had celebrated the American mythic landscape in a poetic image that called for imaginatively transforming the idea bound up in America's past geographical drive West into a many-leveled pursuit of national adventure and mission. . . . The Green Beret in Southeast Asia was . . . one of the specific images in which Kennedy projected his vision of the contemporary American reinvigorating the American errand.[14]

Two years earlier, Alisdair Spark observed that "the Green Beret has proved a consistent focus for popular interest in the Vietnam War."[15] He also noted that "the myth of the Green Beret has served as a vehicle to express the purpose and experience of Vietnam"[16] and that the administration of John F. Kennedy was "where the myth began and was cultivated most assiduously."[17]

Since the myth surrounding the Special Forces was an important part of Kennedy's New Frontier, and since America's involvement in Vietnam was to have such far-reaching consequences for both countries, the president's employment of this myth seems a fitting subject for examination. Further, such an analysis may contribute to the theoretical understanding of mythic criticism, an effort not lacking in heuristic value. As Martha Solomon has pointed out, "The use of myth as a rhetorical strategy deserves closer scrutiny. Questions about when myths are applicable rhetorically, which elements are employed, and why and if they are effective are all obvious avenues for research."[18] This chapter discusses the Green Beret myth and Kennedy's use of it first, by considering the use of the hero myth in rhetoric; second, by examining Kennedy's perception of the policy exigence facing America and the rhetorical exigence arising from it; third, by discussing the specific rhetorical employment of the Special Forces in mythic terms; and fourth, by suggesting some effects of Kennedy's use of this myth.

HERO MYTHS AND RHETORIC

Definitions of myth have been offered by philosophers, theologians, literary critics, anthropologists, and others. With acknowledgement to the work of Dan Nimmo and James Combs,[19] as well as Waldo Braeden,[20] I define myth as a widespread belief existing within a group or culture that has the following characteristics: (1) it is socially constructed, not handed down wholecloth from some outside source; (2) it includes elements both factual and fictional that are mingled together; (3) it serves an emotional or psychological need for those who believe in it; and (4) it typically takes dramatic form as in a story, legend, or poem.

The subjects of myths often conform to patterns or genres, such as those dealing with creation, evil, or the deity.[21] One of the most persistent subjects of myth has been the hero. Hero myths have appeared in such diverse forms as nursery rhymes, dime novels, the classical myths of the ancient Greeks and Romans, and accounts of early Christian saints.[22] Such myths continue today. Nimmo and Combs refer to the

"American monomyth" as an essential part of this country's culture. This term describes the account of a pure, brave, dedicated American hero who defeats evildoers by virtue of his superior skills and high moral purpose. Such figures permeate U.S. popular culture and include such frontier heroes as Davy Crockett and the Lone Ranger, as well as law enforcement figures such as the FBI agent and a host of other detectives, both public and private.[23]

Kenneth Mihalik contends that the rhetorical use of the hero myth can serve three functions: *receptiveness*, which establishes a common rhetorical ground between rhetor and audience; *celebrativeness*, which sets up a standard of achievement and invites others to strive for it; and *potency/transcendence*, which points toward heroism as the mechanism for overcoming obstacles or effecting change. The last function is particularly important here. Mihalik notes, "The purpose of heroism under the potency category . . . is to convince listeners that reality can be transformed."[24] A similar argument is made by Mircea Eliade, who claims that belief in a hero myth allows a person to undertake a difficult task, knowing that a hero has already accomplished a similar, or even more difficult, task in legend.[25] The connection to Vietnam is made explicit by Richard Slotkin, who asks the rhetorical question "*[w]hy are we in Vietnam?*" and concludes "[t]he answer implicit in the myth is, 'We are there because our ancestors were heroes who fought the Indians, and died (rightly or wrongly) as sacrifices for the nation.' "[26]

As will be shown, this is precisely what John F. Kennedy was trying to accomplish in his use of the Green Beret myth: to convince Americans that the Special Forces were archetypal heroes who could defeat the Communist threat in Southeast Asia. But before this issue can be explored, it is necessary to understand how Kennedy and his advisers perceived the world they were facing at the beginning of the 1960s.

JOHN F. KENNEDY: EXIGENCE AND RESPONSE

Lloyd Bitzer has argued that rhetoric occurs in response to an *exigence*—a need or imperfection that is perceived by the rhetor. The rhetor then addresses his or her message to an audience composed of those who have the power to modify the exigence.[27] But some exigences require responses other than rhetoric. In the world of politics and government, leaders often encounter situations that require, first and foremost, the development of policy. Of course, such leaders, especially in democracies, must frequently employ rhetoric to explain and justify their policies—which brings us back to Bitzer's conception. On assuming the presidency, Kennedy perceived a policy exigence and devised a policy to meet it; but the implementation of that policy produced a rhetorical exigence and the president was forced to address that, as well.

Kennedy's perceptions were formed by a number of factors. Some of these came from the decade just past. During the 1950s, China, the most populous nation on Earth, had become a Communist country. Cuba, a country much smaller than China but considerably closer to the United States, had become Communist in 1959. The Soviets had launched the Sputnik satellite in 1957, an event that suggested to many Americans that the Russians might have more determination and better technology than they did.[28] Communist insurgents were active in Vietnam and Laos, and the French were losing a guerrilla war in Algeria.[29]

All of these events resulted in a great deal of discussion and speculation by U.S. opinion leaders as the 1950s became the 1960s. During Nikita Khruschev's visit to the United States in 1959, Walter Lippman wondered in print whether Americans had lost their sense of "great purpose and high destiny" that would allow them to compete successfully with the Communists.[30] Shortly thereafter, George Kennan described the United States as a country "with no highly developed sense of national purpose."[31] Other newspapers and magazines picked up the theme in their editorial pages, and the issue was an important one in the presidential election of 1960. Kennedy's campaign slogan, "Let's get this country moving again," was partly a reference to the economic recession, but it was also an expression of his desire to reinvigorate the American spirit.

Kennedy's perceptions of aggressive Communism were strengthened and given focus in a speech by Khruschev delivered in January 1961. In it, the Soviet premier pledged his country's support to "wars of national liberation" that were being waged, and would increasingly be waged, around the globe.[32] The speech concerned Kennedy greatly, and he read passages from it aloud at his first meeting with the National Security Council. At this meeting the seeds were sown for what was to become Kennedy's policy response to the exigence. The president expressed concisely his view of the exigence and hinted at the forthcoming policy response in a speech given shortly after the fiasco at the Bay of Pigs. He described the exigence this way:

For we are opposed around the world by a monolithic and ruthless conspiracy that relies primarily on covert means for expanding its sphere of influence—on infiltration instead of invasion, on subversion instead of elections, on intimidation instead of free choice, on guerrillas by night instead of armies by day.[33]

Kennedy outlined a vague policy response in the speech. But, in the light of historical hindsight, what he was talking about seems clear. He said: "We intend to profit from this lesson [of Cuba]. We intend to re-examine and re-orient our forces of all kinds—our tactics and our institutions here in this community. We intend to intensify our efforts for a struggle in many ways more difficult than war."[34]

"Counterinsurgency" was the name given to Kennedy's policy of trying to combat the influence of Communist guerrillas through a combination of military and political tactics. It was intended to substitute for the use of large numbers of conventional military forces; Kennedy believed such forces were useless against guerrillas—a view not shared by many senior U.S. military officers.

Thus, the policy exigence described by Kennedy was of hostile Communism on the prowl, seeking to subvert democracy around the world by sponsoring guerrilla wars in Third World countries. His policy response was counterinsurgency. The president also faced a rhetorical exigence stemming from his policy, however. The reasons behind this rhetorical situation require explanation. In theory, Kennedy could have employed these troops in Vietnam without making significant public mention of them. The new policy of counterinsurgency required the Green Berets; it did not, strictly speaking, require the use of the Green Beret myth.

But Kennedy's concerns were not restricted to military policy, and rhetorical, as well as military, strategies were required to address the others. As Gary Wills noted, "The circumstances for using the Special Forces had to be *created*" (Wills' emphasis),[35] and rhetoric played an important part in the creative process. The policy response, counterinsurgency, had to be sold to several audiences. That was the rhetorical exigence that Kennedy faced.

One such audience was Congress. The president gave significant mention to Special Forces in his 1961 "Special Message to Congress on Urgent National Needs."[36] The fact that this speech was presented orally was significant; traditionally, such messages had been sent to Congress in writing. Kennedy's personal appearance was designed to underscore the importance he placed on specific issues, including military preparedness. His choice of Congress as audience is easily understood; he wanted to expand U.S. conventional military forces, including the Green Berets, and he wanted Congress to pay for them.[37]

Another audience for Kennedy's rhetoric of the Green Beret myth was the military itself. When he delivered the commencement address at the U.S. Military Academy, he was addressing more than the army's class of 1962; he was speaking to the entire military command structure.[38] The generals had shown a marked lack of enthusiasm for counterinsurgency in general and for Special Forces in particular.[39] The Joint Chiefs of Staff had even forbidden the wearing of the elite beret until Kennedy personally ordered otherwise. The president wanted support for the Green Berets from the military establishment, but he had had enough military experience to know that merely giving orders was no guarantee they would be carried out. He knew persuasion was necessary.

There was another, related reason. Kennedy wanted to muster Congressional support for counterinsurgency, and he knew the generals had many friends on Capitol Hill. As Loren Baritz pointed out, "JFK believed that if the Joint Chiefs made their opposition to counterinsurgency public, strong Congressional support for them would surely form. . . . It was imperative to keep the Chiefs on his side if possible, but if not, at least quiet."[40] He thus saw the military as important members of his audience.

Public opinion was a major consideration in the formulation of Kennedy's Vietnam policy, as it would be for presidents Johnson and Nixon.[41] Although during Kennedy's administration there was no significant opposition to the commitment of troops to Vietnam, the president was concerned that such sentiments would develop. He told NBC's Huntley and Brinkley that "[w]hat I am concerned about is that Americans will get impatient and say because they don't like events in Southeast Asia or they don't like the government in Saigon, that we should withdraw."[42] Kennedy created and employed the Green Beret myth to develop support for the use of Special Forces in the Vietnam struggle.

The final reason for Kennedy's rhetoric of the Green Beret myth may have been the most important, involving as it did his desire to bolster his credibility with the American people. Several of Kennedy's early efforts in foreign policy had been failures. The abortive Bay of Pigs invasion had been a military and political disaster. Shortly afterward, at the Vienna summit conference with Khruschev, Kennedy thought he had been "beaten up" by the Soviet leader.[43] He worked for the establishment of a pro-Western government in Laos and lost face when Laos declared itself neutral in the East-West power struggle. The result was a perceived twofold problem. The first aspect was Kennedy's desire to restore the credibility he believed he had lost with the electorate. As William Rust pointed out, "To Kennedy Administration officials, the eroding confidence in the President demanded a demonstration of American firmness, particularly in Southeast Asia."[44]

The second aspect of the credibility problem involved America's political right wing. Kennedy thought that, following Cuba, Vienna, and Laos, he was running the risk of being perceived as "soft on Communism" by extreme conservatives. This charge had plagued the Democrats in the 1950s and had helped to usher in a period of anti-Communist hysteria. Kennedy wanted no resurgence of McCarthyism during his administration, and he resolved to take measures to prevent it.[45]

THE GREEN BERETS SOLVE THE RHETORICAL
EXIGENCE

For all intents and purposes, John F. Kennedy created the Green Berets, although the Special Forces were in fact organized in 1952 by order of President Eisenhower. Their original roles were envisioned as the organization, training, and direction of guerrilla forces behind the Iron Curtain in the event of a conventional war between the United States and the Soviet Union. But the program was never given a great deal of attention by the army, and, by the time Kennedy took office, fewer than 2,000 men were active in Special Forces.[46]

Kennedy changed all that quickly. He revitalized the army's Special Forces program and ordered the other services to develop counterinsurgency capabilities. He greatly increased the authorized unit strength of the Special Forces, and he called for research and development of new weapons and equipment for counterinsurgency warfare. Despite the attention given to their strategic value, however, the Special Forces were, above all else, a symbol, "the most public of [Kennedy's] personal initiatives in counterinsurgency."[47] From a rhetorical perspective, counterinsurgency was an abstract concept unlikely to excite much interest or support from the mass public. But the Green Berets were real; they could be seen—and admired. A nation involved in military conflict, even of the "low intensity" variety, needs heroes—and the Special Forces provided prime hero material.[48] As Hellman observed, "The Green Beret would perform a symbolic drama of America's remembered past and dreamed future."[49]

Kennedy made rhetorical use of the Special Forces through two communication channels: manipulation of press accounts and public speeches. The press manipulation was accomplished subtly but effectively. Certainly, journalism in America is relatively free of restraints. The government can neither tell a reporter what to write nor dictate to a publisher what to print. But government can have substantial influence over the press when it wants to. This was more the case during the Kennedy administration than it is today, given such cynicism-inducing events as Johnson's credibility gap and Nixon's Watergate scandal. And when it came to the Special Forces, the government was the sole source of information. Kennedy's people had nearly total control of reporters' access to the Green Berets, and this allowed substantial influence over press accounts.

Kennedy had two specific goals for press coverage of the Green Berets: he wanted his troops to be portrayed as an elite unit and he wanted them to be shown as supremely competent at counterguerrilla warfare.

Kennedy's most conspicuous effort to have the Special Forces depicted as an elite military unit involved the headgear by which these soldiers are popularly known. The green beret had briefly been worn by Special Forces troopers in Europe during the 1950s, but the army command structure had decided that it was inappropriate and forbade its use. The army had a long history of distrust and dislike of elite units. But Kennedy had other ideas. Over the objections of the Joint Chiefs of Staff, he ordered the green beret to be a standard part of the Special Forces uniform, saying, "The Special Forces need something to make them distinctive."[50] Kennedy wanted the Green Berets to be the best troops in the army. Equally important, he wanted them to be *perceived* as the best.[51]

Another way in which the president contributed to the elite image of Special Forces was through selectivity. Kennedy believed in toughness, and he directed the army to make the Special Forces course a demanding one. The rhetorical aim was achieved. *Time* magazine reported that the thirty-eight-week long program was "a killing tenure of unrelieved work and pressure."[52] The failure rate at the Special Warfare School was high, often exceeding 50 percent,[53] and, as a result, those who survived the course and won the right to wear the green beret were described as "uncommon men" and "extraordinary physical specimens."[54]

The news media depiction of the Special Forces as an elite unit had definite rhetorical implications. Under some interpretations of the hero myth, the hero cannot be a common man or woman. The hero, to be perceived as such, must rise above the crowd, must perform deeds of which others are incapable.[55] Elite military units have long given rise to perceptions of heroism, as much from their very selectivity as from anything they actually accomplished militarily.[56] As Eliot Cohen suggested, "Elite units are obvious symbols. Their exploits fit the heroic model of war . . . : they reduce war to terms that a large public can admire and identify with."[57]

Kennedy's other public relations goal for the Special Forces was to have them depicted in the media as experts at counterinsurgency warfare. The Special Warfare School itself provided a principal stimulus to such portrayals. In the fall of 1961, for example, Kennedy had the White House press corps brought down to Fort Bragg, where the Green Berets put on what they called (among themselves) a "Disneyland Show." They demonstrated their skill at unarmed combat and with a variety of weapons. They showed the reporters how to conduct an ambush in the jungle and how to defeat one. The climax of the demonstration featured a Greet Beret with a rocket strapped to his back flying from one side of a pond to the other without getting a foot wet.[58] The quote of a Special Forces trooper who took part in several such "Disneyland" demonstrations may clarify the persuasive aspect of this display. He wrote years later that "[m]uch of the equipment shown, including the rocket, had never been seen before and probably would never be seen again, and much of it had no application to Special Forces anyway."[59]

The purpose of this public relations campaign was to impress the media, and, judging from press reports of that period, it did. The Green Berets, according to *Time* magazine, "can remove an appendix, fire a foreign-made or obsolete gun, blow up a bridge, handle a bow and arrow, sweettalk some bread out of a native in his own language, fashion explosives out of chemical fertilizer, cut an enemy's throat . . . live off the land."[60]

A later issue of *Time* called the Special Forces "the best combat troops in the Army,"[61] and *The Saturday Evening Post* referred to them as the "Harvard Ph.D.s of warfare."[62] An article in *Look* maintained that "Special Forces has proven that it can master the kinds of wars Americans are going to have to learn how to fight."[63] *Popular Science* described the Green Berets as "experts in the dark-of-night techniques of guerrilla warfare" and claimed that "Special Forces men can scrap like jungle cats."[64] Newspaper stories also extolled the virtues of the American counterguerrillas. *The New York Times* reported how a Special Forces "A" team in Vietnam was "arming, training, and organizing the politically listless Rhade tribesmen into a surprisingly effective anti-guerrilla army,"[65] and a story by United Press International described the Green Berets as "a bunch of supermen."[66] Nor were the electronic media immune to the public relations campaign. An NBC news story referred to the Special Forces as "those highly trained men, designed particularly to handle the so-called limited wars."[67] The available evidence supports the conclusion arrived at by George Goodman, who said that "[t]he publicity seemed to focus on the romantic, movie-script ideas of Special Forces."[68]

Clearly, "the increased variety of information media . . . and the refining of public relations techniques makes it easier for publicists to create an heroic image for elite units,"[69] as the Kennedy administration demonstrated in the case of the Special Forces. The popular image of the Green Berets contains two elements that, at first glance, appear to be contradictory, however. One element portrayed the Special Forces soldier as a master of modern military technology. For example, after describing a Special Forces "Disneyland" show, Wills concluded that the predominant message being communicated was "[t]he Americans were coming—savvy as the Viet Cong, and with fancier gadgets."[70]

The other element suggested just the opposite—that the Green Berets did not need technology because they were so tough. Toby Thompson perceived the Special Forces image this way: "It was their primitiveness which attracted. America knew firepower, planes, aircraft carriers, helicopters . . . but Green Berets knew the jungle, blade in hand, knew reliance on a minimum of technology."[71]

On the face of it, this does appear contradictory. The subthemes of myths are not always consistent, however.[72] And this particular image— the strong, tough man who is also a master of weapons technology— fits very well within a fundamental American myth: the image of the frontiersman. As Rushing argued, "From birth to maturity, America has drawn upon the frontier for its mythic identity. . . . Since the beginning, the pioneer spirit has shaped the American dream and infused its rhetoric."[73] The characteristics of the Frontier Hero, as passed on to Americans through their popular myths, feature the two disparate virtues of toughness and technology. As Baritz observed:

The traditional American male, as John Wayne personified him in scores of movies, performs, delivers the goods, is a loner, has the equipment, usually a six-shooter or a superior rifle, to beat the bad guys, and he knows what he is doing. He does not need to depend on others because he can perform, can deliver, and can bring home the bacon.[74]

The ease with which the Green Berets were accepted into the Frontier Hero tradition was aided by both traditional popular culture and the specific popular culture of the early 1960s. Televised frontier heroes such as Paladin, the Lone Ranger, and Wyatt Earp, along with other popular characters, all fit the mold: they were heroes who were physically tough and able to use the technology available to defeat their enemies.[75] This myth is so integral to American life that Kennedy was able to portray the Green Berets as Frontier Heroes without once ever using the term in public. His message was implicit, but clear. In the words of Slotkin:

The terminology of the Myth of the Frontier has become part of our common language, and we do not require an explanatory program to make it comprehensible. We understand quickly and completely the rules of the Cowboy and Indian game, and what it means to invoke it in a place like Vietnam.[76]

John F. Kennedy did not invent the hero myth; that was in place thousands of years before he was born. Nor did he invent the uniquely American myth of the Frontier Hero; it preceded him by more than a hundred years. But he was able, through careful image management, to have the Green Beret portrayed in the media as "a contemporary reincarnation of the western hero,"[77] which made the Special Forces a particularly potent symbol. If Kennedy depicted the world as a New Frontier, then the Green Berets were its New Frontiersmen.

Having successfully encouraged the press to depict the Special Forces as modern Frontier Heroes, Kennedy was able to use his public speeches as vehicles to show how the Green Berets could solve the policy exigence provided by Communist wars of national liberation, thus satisfying the rhetorical exigence, as well. This effort can be seen in both the president's personal rhetoric and the speeches and writings by some of his surrogates.

In an address to Congress two months after assuming office, Kennedy described the policy exigence this way: "Non-nuclear wars, and sub-limited or guerrilla warfare, have since 1945 constituted the most active and constant threat to Free World security."[78] He then proposed the solution: "We must be prepared to make a substantial contribution in the form of strong, highly mobile forces trained in this type of warfare."[79]

Two months later, in his "Special Message to Congress on Urgent National Needs," the pattern was the same: the policy exigence was based on Communist-supported guerrilla warfare, and the policy response was the use of the Green Berets. He referred to "guerrillas striking at night . . . assassins striking alone . . . subversives and saboteurs and insurrectionists, who in some cases control whole areas inside of independent nations."[80] But the problem could be solved: "Our special forces and unconventional warfare units will be increased and re-oriented. . . . New emphasis must be placed on the special skills and languages which are required to work with local populations."[81]

In 1962, Kennedy was the graduation speaker at the U.S. Military Academy. In his address, he again used the same formula of exigence and response. He described for the graduates a new type of war that was being seen around the world: "War by guerrillas, subversives, insurgents, assassins, war by ambush instead of by combat; by infiltration, instead of aggression, seeking victory by eroding and exhausting the enemy instead of engaging him."[82] Then he described for the new officers what their futures might bring: "You may hold a position of command with our special forces, forces which are too unconventional to be called conventional, forces which are growing in number and importance and significance."[83]

On November 22, 1963, in the last speech of his life, Kennedy told the Fort Worth Chamber of Commerce that he had "increased our special counter-insurgency forces which are engaged now in South Viet-Nam by 600 percent," and he reminded its members that "this is a very dangerous and uncertain world."[84]

Surrogates of the president also supported the Special Forces in various forums. In a major speech, Secretary of Defense Robert McNamara pledged that the U.S. would fight Communist-inspired insurgents "[n]ot with massive forces and nuclear weapons, but with companies and squads and individual soldiers."[85] At McNamara's side during the speech was a prime example of the kind of troops to which he was referring: Major General William B. Rosson, commander of the Special Forces.

Presidential Assistant Walt Rostow, one of the architects of Kennedy's counterinsurgency doctrine, gave a speech (approved by the president in advance) to a graduating class of Green Berets at Fort Bragg. He told them, "I salute you, as I would a group of doctors, teachers, economic planners, agricultural experts, civil servants, or those others who are now leading the way in the whole southern half of the globe in fashioning the new nations."[86]

Brigadier General William Yarborough, who succeeded Rosson as head of the Special Forces, argued in print that a Green Beret must be a superb soldier, indeed:

In addition to having the necessary physical and mental development, he must have that firmness of character and purpose that enables him to perform his duty during long periods of isolation under adverse living and climatic conditions. He must be able to bear unusual hardship or suffering.[87]

Clearly, through the use of press manipulation, public speaking, and other means, the Kennedy administration attempted to create for the Special Forces an image of heroism and supreme competence.

EFFECTS, INTENDED AND OTHERWISE

Kennedy's use of the Green Beret myth worked—up to a point. He succeeded in convincing Americans that counterinsurgency would work and that the United States "could successfully intervene in Vietnamese politics"[88] through the use of the Special Forces. A factor strengthening the president's efforts was the lack of media criticism that more contemporary chief executives have come to expect whenever American forces are sent abroad. As J. Fred MacDonald observed, "President Kennedy was moving the United States into the Vietnam War, and American television was practically silent on the matter."[89] The news media had been, for a time, persuaded; they had accepted the Green Beret myth.

Other effects involved the military. The dissemination of the Green Beret myth brought some young men into military service. One young member of the Special Forces explained his reasons for joining in these words: "The mission of the Special Forces already intrigued me. . . . Infiltrating, running in to organize a resistance movement. To free those who were occupied or oppressed. I dug on that."[90] Undoubtedly, many who volunteered for the Special Forces were drawn by the unit's elite image and reputation for heroism.[91] Philip Caputo, a Marine officer in Vietnam, explained how many of his fellow officer trainees had been interested in counterinsurgency, their decision to join the Marines influenced by Kennedy's mythmaking: "The glamorous prince of Camelot had given the new doctrine his imprimatur by sending the first Special

Forces detachments to Vietnam, glamorous figures themselves in their green berets and paratrooper boots."[92] The salutary effects of the myth on military recruitment even survived the president himself. In 1963, author Robin Moore expressed interest in writing a book about the Green Berets, and Kennedy ordered the Special Forces to cooperate. Moore, a civilian, was permitted to go through airborne training and part of the Special Warfare course and to spend six months with a Green Beret detachment in Vietnam. His collection of short stories, *The Green Berets*, appeared in 1965 and sold a large number of copies. So successful was the book in transmitting the Green Beret myth that Army enlistment centers were temporarily flooded. The number of men who joined, in the hope of becoming members of the Special Forces, was so large that the Selective Service system was not required to issue any draft calls during the first four months of 1966.[93]

However impressed some enlisted men and junior officers may have been with the possibilities of counterinsurgency, many senior officers were not. Most of the members of the army's command structure were never enthusiastic about the use of Special Forces. Kennedy could order the generals and admirals to create special warfare units and he persuaded them to avoid public criticism of his counterinsurgency program. But he was never able to mitigate their prejudice against elite units. This becomes important when one considers how Kennedy's use of the Green Beret myth facilitated the escalation of the Vietnam struggle into the major military conflict it became under Presidents Johnson and Nixon.

The subject of whether Kennedy would have curtailed American involvement in Vietnam, had he lived and been elected to a second term, is controversial.[94] His assassination on November 22, 1963, rendered the issue moot. Lyndon Johnson came into office faced with Kennedy's commitment in Vietnam, a commitment largely made possible by Kennedy's skillful use of the Green Beret myth.[95] Lyndon Johnson decided to keep that commitment. But when he asked the generals for advice, they told him that counterinsurgency was not working and that the solution lay in the concentrated application of conventional military force, both on the ground and in the air.[96] Thus was the way paved for escalation. Using the Green Berets as modern manifestations of the Frontier Hero, John Kennedy had opened the door to involvement in Vietnam. Later, Lyndon Johnson kicked the door off its hinges.

In a recent study of American culture and the Vietnam War, Baritz wrote that "[n]ational myths become important to the rest of the world only when they are coupled to national power sufficient to impose one nation's will on another."[97] Clearly, Kennedy was able to attempt the imposition of American power on Vietnam's struggle because of his skillful use of myth. He perceived a problem in the world (Communist-inspired guerrilla warfare) and devised a solution (counterinsurgency).

He presented the same exigence rhetorically to the American people, but he personified the policy in the form of the Special Forces. Kennedy portrayed the Green Berets in ways that Americans could easily understand; the Frontier Hero is basic to American myth, and, hence, to American life. Consequently, the Special Forces became "the major symbol of heroism in the popular culture of American society during the Vietnam War."[98] Kennedy was able to persuade the public—and specific segments thereof, such as the news media and Congress—that these heroes had the "right stuff" for the Vietnam conflict. Consequently, some of the glamour of the Special Forces rubbed off on their creator—the relationship was reciprocal. As Henry Fairlie concluded:

> There was something in the temper of the time, and especially of the American people at the time, which was ready to respond to the [Green Beret] mystique, especially when it found expression in the words and the deeds of so young and so vigorous a President.[99]

For years after Kennedy's death, visitors to Arlington National Cemetery were able to see two objects resting atop his grave. One was the Eternal Flame; the other was a Special Forces green beret.

NOTES

1. W. Lance Bennett, "Myth, Ritual, and Political Control," *Journal of Communication* 30 (1980): 166–179.
2. Don Rice, "Castro's Early Rhetoric: The Myth of the Savior," in *Visions of Rhetoric: History, Theory, and Criticism: Proceedings of the Conference of the Rhetoric Society of America in Arlington, Texas, May 26–June 1, 1986*, ed. Charles W. Kneupper (Arlington, TX: Rhetoric Society of America, 1987), 193–207.
3. Michael McGuire, "Mythic Rhetoric in *Mein Kampf*: A Structuralist Critique," *Quarterly Journal of Speech* 63 (1977): 1–13.
4. Kurt W. Ritter, "The Myth-Making Functions of the Rhetoric of the American Revolution: Francis Hopkinson as a Case Study," *Today's Speech* 23 (1975): 25–31; Catherine L. Albanese, *Sons of the Fathers* (Philadelphia: Temple University Press, 1976), 46–80.
5. Jeff D. Bass and Richard Cherwitz, "Imperial Mission and Manifest Destiny: A Case Study of Political Myth in Rhetorical Discourse," *Southern Speech Communication Journal* 43 (1978): 213–232.
6. John C. Hammerback and Richard J. Jensen, "To 'Make Outrageous Contagious': Abbie Hoffman's Rhetoric of Myth and Media," in *In Search of Justice: The Indiana Tradition in Speech Communication*, ed. Richard J. Jensen and John C. Hammerback (Amsterdam: Rodopi, 1987), 271–283.
7. Robert P. Newman, "Lethal Rhetoric: The Selling of the China Myths," *Quarterly Journal of Speech* 61 (1975): 113–128.
8. Paul D. Erickson, "Daniel Webster's Myth of the Pilgrims," *New England Quarterly* 57 (1984): 44–64.

9. Martha Solomon, "The 'Positive Woman's' Journey: A Mythic Analysis of the Rhetoric of STOP ERA," *Quarterly Journal of Speech* 65 (1979): 262–274.

10. Walter R. Fisher, "Reaffirmation and Subversion of the American Dream," *Quarterly Journal of Speech* 59 (1973): 160–167.

11. Hal W. Fulmer, "A Rhetoric of Oldspeak: Mythic Elements in Presidential Inaugural Addresses 1960–1980," *Rhetoric Society Quarterly* 16 (1986): 299–312.

12. Janice Hocker Rushing, "Ronald Reagan's 'Star Wars' Address: Mythic Containment of Technical Reasoning," *Quarterly Journal of Speech* 72 (1986): 415–433.

13. Janice Hocker Rushing, "Mythic Evolution of 'The New Frontier' in Mass Mediated Rhetoric," *Critical Studies in Mass Communication* 3 (1986): 265–296.

14. John Hellman, *American Myth and the Legacy of Vietnam* (New York: Columbia University Press, 1986), 95.

15. Alasdair Spark, " 'The Soldier at the Heart of the War': The Myth of the Green Beret in the Popular Culture of the Vietnam Era," *Journal of American Studies* 18 (1984): 29–30.

16. Ibid., 30.

17. Ibid.

18. Solomon, 274.

19. Dan Nimmo and James E. Combs, *Subliminal Politics* (Englewood Cliffs, NJ: Prentice-Hall, 1980).

20. Waldo W. Braeden, "Myths in a Rhetorical Context," *Southern Speech Communication Journal* 40 (1975): 113–126.

21. Joseph Campbell, *Myths to Live By* (New York: Bantam Books, 1972).

22. Joseph Campbell, *The Hero with a Thousand Faces* (New York: Pantheon Books, 1949), 340.

23. Nimmo and Combs, 153. Davy Crockett was, of course, a real person, just as the FBI is a real law enforcement organization. The popular myths surrounding both often transcend the historical record to a great degree, however. See, for example, Richard Gid Powers, *G-Men* (Carbondale, IL: Southern Illinois University Press, 1983).

24. Kenneth Mihalik, "The Myth of the Hero as a Rhetorical Strategy," Paper presented at the Annual Meeting of the Speech Communication Association, Denver, CO, November 5–8, 1985, 11.

25. Mircea Eliade, *Myth and Reality*, trans. Willard R. Trask (New York: Harper & Row, 1963), 141.

26. Richard Slotkin, *The Fatal Environment* (New York: Atheneum, 1985), 19.

27. Lloyd Bitzer, "The Rhetorical Situation," *Philosophy and Rhetoric* 1 (1968): 3–4.

28. Rupert Wilkinson, *American Tough* (New York: Perennial Library, 1986), 48.

29. The FLN insurgents in Algeria were not Communists. The Algerian struggle was, however, another example in the early 1960s of a conflict between a Western democracy and Third World indigenous rebels.

30. Cited in Hellman, 42.

31. Ibid.

32. Douglas Blaufarb, *The Counterinsurgency Era* (New York: The Free Press, 1977), 52.

33. John F. Kennedy, " 'The President and the Press,' Address before the American Newspaper Publishers Association, New York City,"in *Public Papers of the Presidents of the United States, 1961* (Washington, DC: Government Printing Office, 1962), 336. This series hereafter referred to as *PPP*.

34. Ibid, 337.

35. Garry Wills, *The Kennedy Imprisonment* (Boston: Little, Brown, 1982), 284.

36. John F. Kennedy, "Special Message to Congress on Urgent National Needs," *PPP, 1961* (Washington, DC: Government Printing Office, 1962), 396–406.

37. Mona Harrington, *The Dream of Deliverance in American Politics* (New York: Alfred A. Knopf, 1986), 208.

38. Charles M. Simpson III, *Inside the Green Berets* (Novato, CA: Presidio Press, 1983), 63–64.

39. William Manchester, *The Glory and the Dream*, 2 vols. (Boston: Little, Brown, 1974), 1280.

40. Loren Baritz, *Backfire* (New York: William Morrow, 1985), 109.

41. Leslie H. Gelb, "The Essential Domino: American Politics and Vietnam," *Foreign Affairs* 50 (1972): 459.

42. Cited in J. Fred MacDonald, *Television and the Red Menace* (New York: Praeger, 1985), 167.

43. Baritz, 113.

44. William J. Rust, *Kennedy in Vietnam* (New York: Charles Scribner's Sons, 1985), 34.

45. James David Barber, *The Presidential Character* (Englewood Cliffs, NJ: Prentice-Hall, 1972), 337.

46. Baritz, 241.

47. Blaufarb, 56.

48. Eliot A. Cohen, *Commandos and Politicians* (Cambridge, MA: Harvard University Center for International Affairs, 1978), 51.

49. Hellman, 53.

50. Quoted in Richard J. Walton, *Cold War and Counterrevolution* (New York: Viking Press, 1972), 173.

51. Louise FitzSimons, *The Kennedy Doctrine* (New York: Random House, 1972), 178.

52. "The American Guerrillas: How to Multiply Small Numbers by an Anti-Communist Factor," *Time*, March 10, 1961, 19.

53. Philip Taubman, "The Secret World of a Green Beret," *The New York Times Magazine*, July 4, 1982, 50.

54. David Halberstam, *The Best and the Brightest* (Greenwich, CT: Fawcett, 1972), 154.

55. Mihalik, 10.

56. Spark, 31.

57. Cohen, 51.

58. Halberstam, 154.

59. Donald Duncan, *The New Legions* (New York: Random House, 1967), 189.

60. "The American Guerrillas: How to Multiply Small Numbers by an Anti-Communist Factor," 19.

61. "The Men in the Green Berets," *Time*, March 1, 1962, 20.

62. Joseph Kraft, "Hot Weapon in the Cold War," *The Saturday Evening Post*, April 28, 1962, 88.

63. Christopher S. Wren, "The Facts behind the Green Beret Myth," *Look*, November 1, 1966, 36.

64. Everett H. Ortner, "Special Forces: The Faceless Army," *Popular Science*, August 1961, 56–57.

65. Homer Bigart, "U.S. Making Army of Vietnam Tribe," *The New York Times*, April 29, 1962, 1.

66. Quoted in George J. W. Goodman, "The Unconventional Warriors," *Esquire*, November 1961, 130.

67. Quoted in MacDonald, 166.

68. Goodman, 129.

69. Cohen, 51.

70. Wills, 251.

71. Toby Thompson, *The 60's Report* (New York: Rawson, Wade, 1979), 142.

72. Braeden, 124.

73. Rushing, "Mythic Evolution of 'the New Frontier' in Mass Mediated Rhetoric," 265.

74. Baritz, 51.

75. MacDonald, 165.

76. Slotkin, 18.

77. Hellman, 45.

78. John F. Kennedy, "Special Message to the Congress on the Defense Budget," *PPP, 1961* (Washington, DC: Government Printing Office, 1962), 232.

79. Ibid., 232.

80. Kennedy, "Special Message to Congress on Urgent National Needs," 397.

81. Ibid., 401.

82. John F. Kennedy, "Remarks at West Point to the Graduating Class of the U.S. Military Academy," *PPP, 1961* (Washington, DC: Government Printing Office, 1963), 453.

83. Ibid., 453.

84. John F. Kennedy, "Remarks at the Breakfast of the Fort Worth Chamber of Commerce," *PPP, 1963* (Washington, DC: Government Printing Office, 1964), 889.

85. Quoted in "The Men in the Green Berets," 19–20.

86. W. W. Rostow, "Guerrilla Warfare in Underdeveloped Areas," in *The Viet-Nam Reader*, ed. Marcus G. Raskin and Bernard B. Fall (New York: Random House, 1965), 116.

87. William P. Yarborough, "Unconventional Warfare: One Military View," *The Annals of the American Academy of Political and Social Science* 341 (1962): 5.

88. Baritz, 322.

89. MacDonald, 166.

90. Quoted in Thompson, 140.

91. William C. Cockerham, "Green Berets and the Symbolic Meaning of Heroism," *Urban Life* 8 (1979): 111.

92. Philip Caputo, *A Rumor of War* (New York: Holt, Rinehart, and Winston, 1977), 16.

93. Hellman, 53.

94. Kenneth O'Donnell, a member of Kennedy's inner circle, has claimed that Kennedy planned to remove U.S. forces from Vietnam after his expected victory in the 1964 election (Rust, x). Kennedy adviser David Powers told me that he believes Kennedy would have terminated American involvement. Others are less certain, including Arthur A. Ekirch, Jr., "Eisenhower and Kennedy: The Rhetoric and the Reality," *Midwest Quarterly* 17 (1976): 285, who says that the proposition that Kennedy would have withdrawn from Vietnam is "doubtful at best." Garry Wills (280–281) claims that Kennedy had made too many commitments to the government of South Vietnam for American disengagement to be feasible, and Kennedy's secretary of state, Dean Rusk, has claimed that the president never mentioned to him any intention to reduce the American presence in Vietnam during the putative second term (cited in Rust, x).

95. Hellman, 66–67.

96. FitzSimons, 202.

97. Baritz, 30.

98. Cockerham, 97.

99. Henry Fairlie, *The Kennedy Promise* (Garden City, NY: Doubleday, 1973), 187.

Chapter Three

"Waist Deep in the Big Muddy": Rhetorical Dimensions of the Tet Offensive

As history shows, it is possible for military events to have implications that go beyond taking ground and inflicting battle casualties. The defeat of Custer's Seventh Cavalry at Little Big Horn became a vital part of the frontier myth that permeates U.S. culture even today; the sinking of the battleship *Maine* by persons unknown prompted public outrage in the United States, leading to a U.S. declaration of war against Spain; the heroic rescue of thousands of stranded British troops from Dunkirk inspired Britons to fight on in the early days of World War II; and the Japanese attack on Pearl Harbor rallied a nation behind a war effort it had previously been unwilling to sponsor.[1]

Likewise, military actions of the Vietnam War possessed rhetorical significance. The Gulf of Tonkin incident, when North Vietnamese patrol boats allegedly attacked ships of the U.S. Navy, formed the basis for President Lyndon Johnson's rhetoric of escalation.[2] The massacre at My Lai, which involved mass murder of civilians by a platoon of U.S. infantry, suggested to some that the brutality of war was not a monopoly of the Communist side. But one military event of the Vietnam War had rhetorical implications yet unconsidered: the Tet offensive of 1968.

This chapter argues that the Communist campaign that occupied the first three months of 1968 had significant rhetorical intentions and resulted in major rhetorical effects. The North Vietnamese had military objectives in the Tet offensive, but they also had a rhetorical goal: to show America that the war was not being won and could not be won at the present level of commitment. This message, embodied in the military activity of the campaign, was developed and transmitted by the American news media to the American public. Ultimately, many Americans came to accept that message, and the result was the downfall of a president.

BRIEF HISTORY OF A CAMPAIGN THAT FAILED—AND SUCCEEDED

Unlike Westerners, who celebrated the New Year on January 1, the Vietnamese observed the Lunar New Year, known as Tet, on January 31. Throughout the long course of the Vietnam War, both the North and South Vietnamese (along with South Vietnam's American allies) had traditionally observed a cease-fire during this holiday period. Minor violations of the truce were often charged by both sides, but, generally, peace reigned for a brief time each year. Tet of 1968 was to be a different story. On January 31, at 3:00 a.m. Vietnamese time, Viet Cong forces in large numbers launched surprise attacks throughout the South. Major targets were larger cities, small towns, and military bases. One group of sappers breached the wall of the U.S. Embassy in Saigon, which had never been successfully attacked before. Several Viet Cong did manage to enter the building in the embassy complex, although the main building remained secure.

The heaviest fighting of the war occurred in the following two months. Viet Cong forces occupied the city of Hue, Vietnam's former capital, and it took U.S. Marines several weeks and many lives to evict them. Across South Vietnam, the Communists were slowly, bloodily driven out of their hastily established urban strongholds. By the end of March, the Tet offensive was effectively over.[3]

Clearly, in military terms, the campaign was a military failure for North Vietnam. A major goal of inspiring a revolt by the South Vietnamese against the Thieu government and its American supporters never materialized. Further, Viet Cong casualties were very high, and many who died were extremely valuable political cadres who would never be replaced.[4] As will be shown, however, the Tet offensive had another, rhetorical, goal that was achieved.

THE MESSAGE IS COMPOSED: THE NORTH VIETNAMESE

North Vietnam leaders devoted considerable thought to planning the Tet offensive. It was, at base, a military campaign, but there were other goals as well. As Jeffrey Milstein noted, "To the North Vietnamese and Viet Cong leaders, American public opinion was of strategic importance to the achievement of their objectives in Vietnam."[5] This was especially true with respect to the Tet offensive, which Hanoi hoped "would shock American opinion and greatly undermine support for the war."[6]

The very existence of the offensive was itself rhetorically significant. For months, President Lyndon Johnson and General William Westmoreland had been claiming that the Viet Cong were finished as a military force in South Vietnam. Widespread guerrilla attacks in the South, they maintained, were unlikely, if not impossible. Tet proved otherwise.

Nor was the timing of the military effort accidental. The North Vietnamese understood American politics, and they knew that 1968 was a presidential election year. Planning began in mid–1967, with a view toward action that would take advantage both of the traditional Tet cease-fire and the U.S. political calendar.[7] It was believed that if the Americans lost faith in their political leaders, they would reject them in favor of others who might be more prone to negotiate peace.

Thus, as Herbert Schandler concluded, "The second purpose of the Communist attack was psychological," which is another way of saying that it was rhetorical.[8] The message that North Vietnam wanted to send to America was simple but powerful. It might be phrased this way: "You cannot win at the present level of engagement. You must either pay a far higher price or negotiate a settlement." Hanoi believed that the first choice was a possibility but that the second was far more likely.[9] As will be shown, the message of the Tet offensive was communicated to the American people very clearly.

THE MESSAGE IS TRANSMITTED: THE NEWS MEDIA

The argument to be developed in this section must be presented clearly. There is no intention to suggest that members of the American news media were acting on behalf of North Vietnam, either as willing agents or as unwitting dupes, in reporting the Tet offensive. Rather, it is contended that members of the news media *believed* the message being sent by the Communists in the campaign and the media transmitted that message to the United States. For purposes of this discussion, it is irrelevant whether the message of Tet—that America could not prevail at the current level of engagement—was *true*.[10] What matters is that the message was *believed* by the correspondents, and they passed it on to the American people, who interpreted it in their own ways.

Clearly, the message was essentially accepted by the media. As E. M. Schreiber pointed out, "If the Tet offensive had a 'message' for the American people, it was that contrary to the Johnson administration's announced interpretations, the war was going badly and a *denouement* favourable [*sic*] to the Americans was not in sight."[11]

Although in strictly military terms the Tet offensive might accurately have been viewed as a defeat for North Vietnam, it was portrayed in the U.S. news media as a major setback for the United States. Indeed, the various components of the news media, the different television networks, wire services, newspapers, and news magazines, were unusually united in their points of view on this issue.[12] The offensive also was a benchmark in the media's coverage of the war. As Daniel Hallin's content analysis shows clearly, following Tet, American reporters and commentators were much more inclined to be critical of the conduct of the war, although this criticism never involved American political institutions or the central values underlying the conflict, such as anti-Communism.[13]

For more than two months, the Tet offensive was a staple of the television news diet in the United States. During this period, the nightly news programs of CBS and NBC were seen by near-record numbers of viewers, and the war was the dominant story night after night. Not only did news reports about the war reach a peak but also certain types of reporting increased dramatically. Commentary about the news by reporters and anchors more than doubled during Tet from previous levels and then fell back again once the offensive was over.[14]

There were three reasons for this intense media coverage of the Tet offensive. One was simple accessibility. Previously, the Viet Cong had fought a guerrilla war, emphasizing hit-and-run tactics and eschewing pitched battles whenever possible. Such activities were very hard for network news teams to find and film. The war correspondents and crews in Vietnam had a title for stories reporting this activity: "The Wily VC Got Away Again."[15] But during Tet, the news teams based in Saigon and other Vietnamese cities did not have to ride helicopters to find the elusive enemy; in many cases, all they had to do was walk down the street to the nearest firefight. As a result, combat footage was shown on America's television screens with unprecedented frequency.

A second reason involved the type of reporters who were covering the Tet campaign. For some time prior to the offensive, many reporters based in Vietnam had been cabling their editors back home that the administration was exaggerating its successes against the Viet Cong, but these reports were generally not taken seriously. The correspondents were too far from the editorial offices to make their case convincingly, and they were often regarded as being too inexperienced to assess the situation accurately. Once Tet began, the networks and publications began to send to Vietnam their journalistic "heavy weights," such as Walter Cronkite. The presence of these experienced, respected reporters guaranteed that their stories would be treated seriously and given wide exposure.[16]

The final reason that the Tet offensive received so much news coverage was the drama inherent in the campaign itself. Tet involved heavy fighting and high American casualties. Further, as will be shown, the campaign did not lack for individual dramatic moments. Journalism, especially television journalism, thrives on drama; consequently, the journalists thrived on Tet.

MESSAGE COMPONENTS: NEWS, ICONOGRAPHY, AND MYTH

Edwin Diamond wrote that "the *iconography* of Vietnam—how it was pictured—helped determine the direction of American policy."[17] An icon is, of course, an image, and "iconography" thus refers to the creation of images. The iconography of the Vietnam War, as created by the news media, changed drastically with the Tet offensive and had considerable impact on American policy.

The reason that the shift in iconography was so important is that it began the process of *demythification*—the challenging or debunking of myths. Both Loren Baritz and John Hellman contend that myth was at the heart of American involvement in Vietnam. Baritz wrote of the American conception of our country as a "city on a hill," that is, an entity that must be an example to the rest of the world, bringing our wisdom to those less fortunate and less wise.[18] Hellman claims that "Americans entered Vietnam with certain expectations that a story, a distinctly American story, would unfold."[19] Certain icons shown to the American people during the Tet offensive called the prevailing myths into question, however. As Hellman noted, "Such images did not correspond to the roles that the national myth ascribed to the American, his noble native ally, and their mutual enemy."[20]

The first image to be analyzed appeared in a photograph in *Life* magazine. In this photo, American embassy official George Jacobson was shown leaning out of his bedroom window at the U.S. Embassy in Saigon with a pistol in his hand. This picture, and others like it, served an important demythification function. It flew in the face of what President Johnson, his spokesmen, and his generals had been saying for months— that the war was under control, that the Viet Cong had been eliminated as an effective force, and that victory was just a matter of time.[21] Jack Valenti, a friend of Johnson, recalled his own reaction to the image from Saigon: "When you see Viet Cong . . . 10 feet from the door of the U.S. embassy before they were finally killed, somebody said, 'My God, if they can get that close to the embassy, the war is over!' "[22] Hugh Sidey, who was a columnist for *Life* at the time, thought the message communicated by this icon was this: "Here you have a handful of troops that can bring explosives and attack the American embassy, and then [Johnson's people] claim that they are winning this war . . . and we just said it's obvious things are worse than anybody knows."[23] The myth of Viet Cong decline leading to imminent American victory was effectively undermined.

The second important image to come out of the Tet offensive existed in two forms: a still photograph and a segment of film. The photo was printed in most major American newspapers, and the film was seen by about twenty million people on NBC's evening news program, "The Huntley-Brinkley Report."[24] The image was of Brigadier General Nguyen Ngoc Loan, commander of the South Vietnamese National Police, putting a bullet into the head of a captured and bound Viet Cong. The story of this incident has become known in some circles as "Rough Justice in a Saigon Street."[25] For reasons of "taste," NBC trimmed a few seconds off the end of the film before broadcast to eliminate footage of blood spurting from the head of the dying Viet Cong. The photograph, which depicted the instant of the bullet's impact, won photographer Eddie Adams the Pulitzer Prize. The icon did Johnson's war effort no good.

This image of the execution of a helpless prisoner was demythifying in that it called into question the administration's claims that South Vietnam was really an ally worth defending. To some, the picture and film "encapsulated the corruption of the South Vietnamese government and military," but to others they were "arguably the turning point of the war."[26] This brutal image, communicated to millions of Americans, "seemed to many people to confirm the suspicion that this was a 'wrong war' on the 'wrong side.' "[27]

The third icon was only a quotation taken from an Associated Press wire story, but it has been called "the most widely quoted remark of the war."[28] After most of a Mekong Delta village called Ben Tre had been deliberately destroyed by American artillery fire, the American officer who had called in the shelling on the village told the AP reporter, "It became necessary to destroy the town in order to save it."[29] The wide circulation of this remark served a demythifying function in a most fundamental way. The myth it challenged was the one that said the Vietnam War made sense. The line "encapsulated the American dilemma in Vietnam, and . . . struck a raw nerve in the body politic at home"; it also "caused many to question the purpose of our being [in Vietnam]."[30] Certainly, the notion that American policy in Vietnam was not based on logic was supported by other news reports following Tet. As Hallin reports, the theme that "the war is rational" largely disappeared from news stories about Vietnam during and after the offensive and was replaced by those stressing the futility of particular actions and battles.[31]

The Tet offensive was not the only event to evoke images that challenged the myths concerning U.S. involvement in Vietnam. But Tet is important because so many disturbing icons were produced within so short a time. This demythification process had serious political implications. When major national myths are undermined, the result is often politically important. As Todd Gitlin observed of the Tet offensive, "A nation that commits itself to myth is traumatized when reality bursts through—in living color."[32]

MESSAGE COMPONENTS: MEDIA OPINION LEADERS

The images coming out of the Tet offensive and into America's homes via "hard news" reports were not the only vehicles communicating the essential message of Tet. Influential persons within the media establishment also took up the refrain. As Don Oberdorfer noted, "The oracles of American society, the commentators, editorial writers and leaders of private America, many of whom had been uneasy and uncertain before, [during Tet] became convinced that the war was being lost or, at the very best, could not be won."[33]

Chief among these sages was Walter Cronkite, the most respected journalist in the United States. For years, Cronkite had accepted the administration's view of the war. But once Tet had begun, Cronkite decided to go to Vietnam and see for himself. While there, he talked with U.S. government officials, consulted with his CBS colleagues and other journalists, and observed the fighting personally. Cronkite returned to New York with a lot of film and a new perspective. On the evening of February 27, 1968, CBS broadcast an hour-long program, "Who, What, When, Where, Why: Report from Vietnam by Walter Cronkite." Near the end of the hour, after the battlefield footage and the film interviews with generals and infantrymen, Cronkite concluded with what he called some "personal observations." He said, in part:

To say that we are closer to victory today is to believe, in the face of the evidence, the optimists who have been wrong in the past. To suggest we are on the edge of defeat is to yield to unreasonable pessimism. To say that we are mired in stalemate seems the only realistic, yet unsatisfactory, conclusion. . . . It is increasingly clear to this reporter that the only rational way out then will be to negotiate, not as victors, but as honorable people who lived up to their pledge to defend democracy, and did the best they could.[34]

The immediate effects of Cronkite's broadcast on public opinion are difficult to estimate, but the immediate effect on the president was clear. After watching Cronkite's broadcast, Johnson commented to his press secretary, "If we've lost Walter Cronkite, we're going to lose a whole lot of people."[35] "It was," said David Halberstam, "the first time in American history a war had been declared over by an anchorman."[36]

A few weeks later, the NBC news staff chimed in on the chorus. "The Frank McGee Sunday Report" was expanded to a full hour for the March 10 broadcast. The program's content contrasted the optimistic predictions of Johnson and his advisers with the bloody realities of Tet. At the end, McGee concluded, "The war, as the administration has defined it, is being lost." Echoing one of the icons of the Tet offensive, he said, "Laying aside all other arguments, the time is at hand when we must decide whether it is futile to destroy Vietnam in order to save it."[37]

Nor were radio journalists idle during this period. If anything, radio news commentary was more critical of Johnson and the war effort than was its television counterpart. One prominent voice was that of David Brinkley, a man not unknown to television viewers. In his syndicated radio commentary of February 15, he referred to a familiar image of Tet, saying: "For either a hawk or dove it is hard to see any point in continuing the war at its present level since it's achieving nothing. It actually is doing harm. It is destroying South Vietnam in the process of saving it."[38]

Many print journalists also became critical of Johnson's handling of the war. *Newsweek* editorialized that "a reappraisal of the U.S. involvement in Vietnam in the light of the Tet offensive" was called for and concluded that the president's refusal to change his strategy was nothing but "a short prescription for further American anguish and humiliation."[39] A week earlier, *Newsweek* columnist Walter Lippman had called for a phased withdrawal from Vietnam, combined with American negotiations with Hanoi. *Time, Life,* and *The Wall Street Journal* also declared their opposition to Johnson's policies in Vietnam.

Clearly, the message embodied in the Tet offensive by North Vietnam was carried very effectively to the American people: at the current level of engagement, America could not win. News stories, especially those carrying demythifying images, and media opinion leaders supported this view—not because the journalists were disloyal Americans, but because they believed the message to be true. The North Vietnamese and Viet Cong had shown by deeds what Lyndon Johnson had been denying with words. The message was received by the American public, and various segments of that public responded in important ways.

THE MESSAGE IS RECEIVED: AMERICA REACTS

The effects that the Tet offensive had on Americans can be discussed in several different ways. One useful approach is offered by public opinion polls; examination of this data will show that Lyndon Johnson was severely hurt by Tet.

During 1967 and 1968, the Gallup Organization asked Americans whether they considered themselves "hawks," people who wanted to increase the war effort, or "doves," those who wanted to decrease the U.S. commitment. The first measurement after Tet began, taken in early February 1968, showed an increase in the number of self-described hawks. That number dropped by 20 percent, however, in the two months that followed.[40] One social scientist has called this shift "probably the largest and most important change in public opinion during the entire war."[41]

Other measures of public sentiment show a similar decline in support for President Johnson. During the Tet offensive, his approval rating reached its lowest level ever, with only 26 percent of those polled approving of the way he was doing his job.[42] The number who approved of his handling of the war declined significantly, as did the number who thought the United States was making progress in Vietnam.[43] The overall effect was well summarized by Godfrey Hodgson, who concluded, "After three years of war, roughly one American out of every five changed his or her mind about it in a single month. That is one crude measure of the effect of Tet."[44]

Significant individuals and groups in America were also influenced by the Tet offensive, although it is difficult to determine whether they were influenced by the campaign itself, the media depictions thereof, the public opinion reactions, or some combination of these. In any case, Tet was what Aristotle would call the "first cause."

One group responding to the Tet offensive consisted of the doves in the U.S. Congress, especially the Senate. Paul Burstein and William Freudenburg found that, generally, Senate voting on Vietnam-related legislation tended to become less supportive of the administration as combat deaths increased.[45] As noted, American casualties during Tet were the highest of the war, reaching more than 500 deaths per week at peak. More specifically, Herbert Schandler noted that "[t]he Tet attacks confirmed many senators' doubts about the direction and costs of the American effort in Vietnam and also brought similar doubts to many fence-sitters and supporters of the war."[46]

The opposition of two senators went beyond debating and casting votes. Eugene McCarthy of Minnesota and Robert Kennedy of New York decided to challenge Johnson for the 1968 Democratic presidential nomination.

McCarthy had long been a dove in the Senate, and, after Tet began, he decided to take more direct action to end the war—by seeking the presidency himself. Vietnam was his primary issue. In an early campaign speech, McCarthy made a number of references that appear to have sprung from the Tet offensive:

In 1966, in 1967, and now again in 1968, we hear the same hollow claims of programs and victory. For the fact is that the enemy is bolder than ever, while we must steadily enlarge our own commitment. The Democratic Party in 1964 promised "no wider war." Yet the war is getting wider every month. Only a few months ago we were told that 65 percent of the population [of South Vietnam] was secure. Now we know that even the American Embassy is not secure.[47]

In the 1968 New Hampshire primary, a contest traditionally regarded as an augury by political experts, McCarthy challenged Johnson and came in second by a margin of less than three hundred votes. For a sitting president to do so poorly in New Hampshire was, at the time, unprecedented. Thereafter, McCarthy was seen as a real threat to Johnson, and those threats began to multiply when Robert Kennedy entered the race for the Democratic nomination. Kennedy had initially been reluctant to run; his long-standing animosity toward Johnson was well known, and the senator did not want to be accused of attacking the president and splitting the party for personal reasons. But after New Hampshire, it was clear to Kennedy that Johnson was politically vulnerable, and that any potential party splitting had already been done by McCarthy. For Kennedy, too, the war was a major issue, and the Tet offensive was a frequent point of reference. "Our enemy," he said, "savagely striking at will across all of South Vietnam, has finally shattered the mask of official illusion with which we have concealed our true circumstances, even from ourselves."[48]

Clearly, the Tet offensive was instrumental in both McCarthy's and Kennedy's decisions to enter the race. E. M. Schreiber concluded that, without the public reaction to Tet, McCarthy's campaign would never have achieved political significance.[49] James Rowe, who had been helping to run Johnson's campaign effort in New Hampshire, concluded after the primary that "the Tet offensive by the Viet Cong is the cause of all this, including the popularity of McCarthy and the entry of Kennedy. It came as a great shock to the American people."[50]

Other individuals who did not themselves aspire to political office were also encouraged by Tet. Antiwar protesters were inspired to new determination by the Viet Cong campaign. Some youthful opponents of the war cut their long hair, wore conventional clothing, and went "Clean for Gene," campaigning for McCarthy in New Hampshire and elsewhere. Although antiwar protesters may have had little or no impact on ending the war and may even have been counterproductive by hardening middle-class resistance, the images coming out of the Tet offensive, along with the new political problems for Lyndon Johnson, breathed new life into the antiwar movement.

All of this was not lost on the president's advisers. Johnson had put together an informal group, called by some administration insiders "the Wise Old Men," to counsel him on Vietnam. The coterie consisted of several recent tenants of high government office, such as former cabinet members, retired generals, and ex-ambassadors, as well as some members of the business community. Johnson called them together periodically when he wanted advice from those not already committed to the administration's policies. In late March 1968, the president convened the "Wise Old Men," and the word they gave him was grim. A significant majority held that the war could not be won as it was being waged; further, they said that public support for the war was eroding steadily and would continue to do so.[51] They, too, had accepted the message of

Tet. The prevailing view of the group was well put by McGeorge Bundy, who had been John Kennedy's national security adviser. He shared the view that "the sentiment in the country on the war has shifted very heavily since the Tet offensive. . . . A great many people—even very determined and loyal people—have begun to think that Vietnam really is a bottomless pit."[52]

For months, Johnson had been resisting the message embodied in the Tet offensive and its media coverage. His public rhetoric during most of the period was designed to minimize the significance of the Communist effort and to reiterate his faith in his own policy. In his first press conference after Tet burst on the scene, the president maintained that "the stated purposes of the general uprising have failed."[53] Later in the press conference, in response to a question regarding whether American strategy would be reassessed in light of Tet, Johnson responded, "As far as changing our basic strategy, the answer would be no."[54] Two weeks later, a reporter asked Johnson if he was considering an increase in U.S. troop strength for Vietnam, to which the president replied, "Yes, we give thought to that every day. We never know what forces will be required there."[55] The next day, speaking to members of the army's 82nd Airborne Division at Fort Bragg, North Carolina, Johnson characterized the Tet offensive by saying, "In [the enemy's] first attempt three weeks ago, he failed. He did inflict terrible wounds on the people, and he took terrible losses himself."[56]

On March 12, Johnson presided over a White House ceremony at which two marines who had fought in Vietnam the prior year were awarded the Congressional Medal of Honor. In his remarks, the president seemed to show an awareness of the growing criticism of his war policy, although he evinced no inclination to accept it. He said:

This is an anxious time for America. It calls for every fiber of our courage, every source of our intelligence, every capacity for sound judgment that the American people can summon—and that the American people possess.

I think if we are steady, if we are patient, if we do not become the willing victims of our own despair, if we do not abandon what we know is right when it comes under mounting challenge—we shall never fail.[57]

Nine days later, in a speech given to the first class to graduate from the Vietnam Training Center set up by the Foreign Service Institute, Johnson stuck to his guns—literally. He discussed Tet at some length, saying, in part, "When the enemy unleashed his savage attack over the Tet holidays, he thought that he would crack the will of the Vietnamese people. But he was wrong."[58] In short, Johnson's approach was that described by one of his advisers, Townsend Hoopes: "The President's basic reaction to the Tet offensive was to convince himself anew that the war was a test of wills between parties of equal interest."[59]

Johnson also used the rhetoric of surrogates to support his position. During the early weeks of Tet, the secretaries of state and defense were fixtures on such television interview shows as "Meet the Press" and "Face the Nation," defending the administration's war policies and pooh-poohing its critics. The president also ordered General Westmoreland, commander of all U.S. forces in Vietnam, personally to conduct a press briefing at least once each day.[60]

But eventually all of the individuals and groups who had been affected by the iconography of the Tet offensive—the media opinion leaders, the doves in Congress, McCarthy, Kennedy, the Wise Old Men, and, most especially, the mass American public—convinced Johnson that his policy in Vietnam was a failure. It might have worked militarily, but it was not succeeding politically or rhetorically. In a democracy, the last two forms of success are most important. Johnson had been playing in the political poker game long enough to know when to cash in his chips.

On March 31, he gave a major address about Vietnam over national television and radio. Its contents were surprising to many. Johnson announced that he was drastically curtailing American bombing of North Vietnam, and he offered unconditional peace talks with Hanoi. But the biggest surprise came near the end of the speech, when he announced, "I shall not seek, and I will not accept, the nomination of my party for another term as your President."[61]

To say that the Tet offensive brought an end to the presidency of Lyndon Johnson is to oversimplify. Public opinion had been gradually turning against the war for more than a year preceding the Communist surprise attack. But the Tet offensive was a watershed, a point beyond which many Americans were not willing to go—at least, not with Johnson leading the way.

Clearly, the public reaction following Tet did not necessarily constitute a peace movement. Many Americans still believed the war could be won; they simply did not trust Johnson to secure the victory. Of those who voted for McCarthy in New Hampshire, a large number did so as much out of dissatisfaction with the president as they did out of support for the senator; many who supported McCarthy in that primary also considered themselves to be hawks on the war.[62]

In a sense, Johnson was the victim of a cruel irony. Tet *was* a significant military defeat for the Communists. They failed to achieve their major military and political objectives, and they suffered tremendous casualties. But another casualty of Tet was Johnson's credibility. He and his administration had been saying for more than a year that America was winning the war and that the Communist forces were on the run. The Tet offensive showed this to be blatantly untrue, and the political fallout was lethal. In Gitlin's words, "No more devastating criticism can be made of a president, whatever his policies, than that he lies."[63] Further, the iconographic depictions coming out of the Tet offensive, so different from those preceding them, challenged the American mythology that had grown up around the war effort. Americans had believed that the U.S. embassy in Saigon, the symbol of American commitment, was sacrosanct—until the Viet Cong showed otherwise. The myth held that the South Vietnamese were humanitarian democrats until General Loan showed his blatant disregard for both human life and due process. The broadest myth, perhaps that on which all the others were based, said that U.S. involvement in Vietnam was founded on logic and good sense. Then a soldier explained how "[w]e had to destroy the village in order to save it," and good sense was perceived to be absent without leave from Vietnam.

The January 11, 1988, issue of *Time* magazine featured a cover story retrospective of the year 1968, "[t]he year that shaped a generation." The article discussed seven major events of that tumultuous year, including the Tet offensive. According to Lance Morrow, "Tet was a defeat for the Communists. But . . . illusion triumphed over reality. America, and much of the rest of the world, regarded Tet as shocking proof that the war was a disaster for the U.S., unwinnable."[64]

From the North Vietnamese perspective, the Tet offensive was a military fiasco and a failed attempt to foment rebellion in the South. But, as rhetoric, it was a significant success.

NOTES

1. Richard Slotkin, *The Fatal Environment* (New York: Atheneum, 1985): Nicholas Harman, *Dunkirk: The Patriotic Myth* (New York: Simon and Schuster, 1980).

2. Richard A. Cherwitz, "Lyndon Johnson and the 'Crisis' of Tonkin Gulf: A President's Justification of War," *Western Journal of Speech Communication* 42 (1978): 93–104.

3. This discussion of the history of the Tet Offensive owes much to Don Oberdorfer, *Tet!* (Garden City, NY: Doubleday, 1971).

4. Daniel C. Hallin, *The "Uncensored War"* (New York: Oxford University Press, 1986).

5. Jeffrey S. Milstein, "The Vietnam War from the 1968 Tet Offensive to the 1970 Cambodian Invasion: A Quantitative Analysis," in *Mathematical Approaches to Politics*, ed. H. R. Alker, Jr., K. W. Deutsch, and A. H. Stoetzel (San Francisco: Jossey-Bass, 1973), 62.

6. Douglas S. Blaufarb, *The Counterinsurgency Era* (New York: The Free Press, 1977), 262.

7. Oberdorfer, 52.

8. Herbert Y. Schandler, *The Unmaking of a President* (Princeton, NJ: Princeton University Press, 1977), 78.

9. Douglas Pike, *War, Peace, and the Viet Cong* (Cambridge, MA: MIT Press, 1969), 140–141.

10. For contrasting views on the validity of this message, see Peter Braestrup, *Big Story*, 2 vols. (Boulder, CO: Westview Press, 1977); and Peter Arnett, "Tet Coverage: A Debate Renewed," *Columbia Journalism Review* 16 (January–February 1978): 44–47.

11. E. M. Schreiber, "Anti-war Demonstrations and American Public Opinion on the War in Vietnam," *British Journal of Sociology* 27 (1976): 227.

12. Dan Nimmo and James E. Combs, *Mediated Political Realities* (New York: Longman, 1983), 167–68.

13. Daniel C. Hallin, "The Media, the War in Vietnam, and Political Support: A Critique of the Thesis of an Oppositional Media," *Journal of Politics* 46 (1984): 6.

14. Hallin, The *"Uncensored War,"* 169.

15. David Halberstam, *The Best and the Brightest* (Greenwich, CT: Fawcett, 1972), 787.

16. Herbert J. Gans, *Deciding What's News* (New York: Vintage Books, 1980), 135.

17. Edwin Diamond, *The Tin Kazoo: Television, Politics, and the News* (Cambridge, MA: MIT Press, 1975), 123.

18. Loren Baritz, *Backfire* (New York: William Morrow, 1985), 33.

19. John Hellman, *American Myth and the Legacy of Vietnam* (New York: Columbia University Press, 1986), x.

20. Ibid., 89.

21. Michael Mandelbaum, "Vietnam: The Television War," *Daedalus* 111 (1982): 159.

22. Linda Ellerbee, Ray Gandolf, and Edward Hersh, "Winds of Change—Winter, 1968," "Our World" [transcript of television program] (New York: Journal Graphics, 1987), 4.

23. Ibid.

24. Oberdorfer, 170.

25. George A. Bailey and Lawrence W. Lichty, "Rough Justice on a Saigon Street: A Gatekeeper Study of NBC's Tet Execution Film," *Journalism Quarterly* 49 (1972): 221.

26. Kathleen J. Turner, *Lyndon Johnson's Dual War* (Chicago: University of Chicago Press, 1985), 218; Nancy Zaroulis and Richard Sullivan, *Who Spoke Up?* (Garden City, NY: Doubleday, 1984), 151.

27. Godfrey Hodgson, *America in Our Time* (Garden City, NY: Doubleday, 1976), 356; and Oberdorfer, 170.

28. Barbara W. Tuchman, *The March of Folly* (New York: Alfred A. Knopf, 1984), 349.

29. Quoted in Hodgson, 356.

30. Zaroulis and Sullivan, 151; Schandler, 81.

31. Hallin, The *"Uncensored War,"* 176–177.

32. Todd Gitlin, *The Whole World Is Watching: Mass Media in the Making and Unmaking of the New Left* (Berkeley, CA: University of California Press, 1980), 299.

33. Oberdorfer, 238.

34. Quoted in Braestrup, vol. 2, 188–189.

35. Quoted in Ellerbee, Gandolf, and Hersh, 7.

36. Halberstam, 514.

37. Quoted in Oberdorfer, 273.

38. Quoted in J. Fred MacDonald, *Television and the Red Menace* (New York: Praeger, 1985), 243.

39. "Needed: The Courage to Face the Truth," *Newsweek*, March 18, 1968, 39.

40. John E. Mueller, *War, Presidents and Public Opinion* (New York: John Wiley and Sons, 1973), 106.

41. Howard Schuman, "Two Sources of Antiwar Sentiment in America," *American Journal of Sociology* 78 (1972): 515.

42. Baritz, 186.

43. E. M. Schreiber, "Anti-War Demonstrations and American Public Opinion on the War in Vietnam," *British Journal of Sociology* 27 (1976): 227.

44. Hodgson, 357.

45. Paul Burstein and William Freudenburg, "Changing Public Policy: The Impact of Public Opinion, Antiwar Demonstrations, and War Costs on Senate Voting on Vietnam War Motions," *American Journal of Sociology* 84 (1978): 116.

46. Schandler, 206.

47. Quoted in Todd Gitlin, *The Sixties: Years of Hope, Days of Rage* (New York: Bantam Books, 1987), 299.

48. Ibid., 300.

49. Schreiber, "American Politics and the Vietnam Issue: Demonstrations, Votes, and Public Opinion," 209.

50. Quoted in Turner, 237.

51. Oberdorfer, 308.

52. Quoted in Turner, 243.

53. Lyndon B. Johnson, "The President's News Conference of 2 February 1968," in *Public Papers of the Presidents of the United States: Lyndon B. Johnson, 1968–69* (Washington, DC: Government Printing Office, 1970), 155. This source cited hereafter as *PPP*.

54. Ibid., 156.

55. Lyndon B. Johnson, "The President's News Conference of 16 February 1968," in *PPP*, 237.

56. Lyndon B. Johnson, "Remarks at Fort Bragg, North Carolina, 17 February 1968," in *PPP*, 239.

57. Lyndon B. Johnson, "Remarks Upon Presenting the Medal of Honor to Maj. Robert J. Modrzejewski and 2nd Lt. John J. McGinty, III, USMC, 12, March 1968," in *PPP*, 377.

58. Lyndon B. Johnson, "Remarks to the First Graduating Class at the Foreign Service Institute's Vietnam Training Center, 21 March 1968," in *PPP*, 424.

59. Townsend Hoopes, *The Limits of Intervention* (New York: David McKay, 1969), 147.

60. Turner, 220.

61. Lyndon B. Johnson, "The President's Address to the Nation Announcing Steps to Limit the War in Vietnam and Reporting His Decision Not to Seek Reelection, 31 March 1968," in *PPP*, 476.

62. Oberdorfer, 276–277.

63. Gitlin, *The Sixties: Years of Hope, Days of Rage*, 299.

64. Lance Morrow, "1968: Like a Knife Blade, the Year Severed Past from Future," *Time*, January 11, 1988, 20.

Chapter Four

Nixon and the Silent Majority: The Rhetoric of Shared Values

Richard Nixon's November 3, 1969, address to the nation on the Vietnam War, commonly known as the "silent majority" speech, has probably been the focus of more critical scrutiny than any of his other public utterances, with the possible exceptions of the 1952 "Checkers" speech and his resignation address in 1974. Nixon's call to the members of the "great silent majority" to make themselves heard has been examined from a variety of critical perspectives, each of which adds something to our understanding of the speech, the man, and the occasion. Robert P. Newman characterizes the speech as an effort by Nixon to secure the support of those who had voted for George Wallace in the 1968 presidential election without driving away the moderate conservatives who were Nixon's main constituency.[1] Karlyn Kohrs Campbell analyzes the "silent majority" address using criteria developed from the speech itself. She concludes that, contrary to the standards that Nixon seems to call for, his speech was neither true, credible, unifying, or ethical.[2] Forbes Hill brings the perspective of neo-Aristotelian criticism to the speech and finds the address to be a success on those terms.[3] Finally, Herman Stelzner discusses Nixon's address as being squarely within the tradition of a venerable literary genre, the quest story.[4]

None of these studies seems to provide a satisfactory explanation, however, for the ways that Nixon's speech functioned for his audience. The speech was widely popular: the flood of phone calls and telegrams in the hours immediately after the speech was overwhelmingly supportive of the president—as well they should have been, since many of these responses were orchestrated by Republican party personnel around the country who were acting under the orders of Nixon staffers.[5]

Other opinion measures, less amenable to manipulation, also showed a strong positive reaction to the address. A Gallup Poll taken immediately after the speech showed that 77 percent of those surveyed agreed with Nixon's assessment. Further, the next measurement of the president's "approval rating," taken two weeks after the speech, showed a whopping 12 percent increase, bringing Nixon to a 68 percent approval figure, his highest rating to that point.[6]

Nixon's "silent majority" speech clearly touched something within the nation's psyche. This occurred, I argue, because his message incorporated a number of fundamental American myths. He showed his audience members that they should believe in him because he believed the same things they did. He spoke of their myths, he embraced their values, and then he asked for their support. They gave it to him with enthusiasm—at least, for a while.

Robert Reich contends that political rhetoric in this country inevitably comes down to "myth-based morality tales that determine when we declare a fact to be a problem, how policy choices are characterized, how the debate is framed. These are the unchallenged subtexts of political discourse."[7] He also says that American cultural mythology is composed of four "morality tales": the mob at the gates, the triumphant individual, the benevolent community, and the rot at the top.[8]

THE MOB AT THE GATES

This cultural myth actually has something to say about those on both sides of the gate: the good people within and the enemy outside. The people inside the gate, protected by the city walls, are always understood to be "us." The fierce enemy outside is, inevitably, portrayed as "them."

The entity within the gate is usually considered to be America itself, "a beacon light of virtue in a world of darkness, a small island of freedom and democracy in a perilous sea."[9] Subgroups within the nation may use the myth to refer to themselves, as when Elijah Muhammed of the Nation of Islam used to preach to his people that "[t]he white man is a devil," but it usually depicts the nation as a whole.

The principal focus of the myth is the enemy, the forces gathered outside. After all, we generally know who "we" are, but the nature and composition of the enemy may need to be described. At various times, the enemy has been, among others, the Indians, the abolitionists, the secessionists, Europeans colonizing Latin America, the Nazis, the Communists (both foreign and domestic), and the Iraqis.[10]

In the "silent majority" speech, Nixon's perception of the "mob at the gates" was presented clearly. The mob consisted of those who demonstrated against the war in Vietnam. They carried placards that said things like " 'Lose in Vietnam, bring the boys home.' " They were a "minority," but they wanted immediate withdrawal of all U.S. forces from Vietnam, a view that they "tr[ied] to impose . . . on the Nation by mounting demonstrations in the street." They were a "vocal minority," and they sought to achieve their goal despite "reason and the will of the majority." If they were to succeed, then "this Nation has no future as a free society."[11] Further, by their demonstrations, these young people sent a message to Hanoi that the United States is far from united in support of the president's policies in Vietnam. This hurt the chances for peace, since "the more divided we are at home, the less likely the enemy is to negotiate at Paris." The ultimate effect of antiwar protest, intended or not, could be "to defeat or humiliate the United States."[12]

That Nixon should portray the antiwar movement as the nation's enemy is not surprising, for he certainly regarded it as *his* enemy. Nixon had long perceived his public life as a series of struggles (or "crises"), and one cannot have a battle without a foe. At various times, he saw the enemy as the press, the Communists, and the Congress. During the Vietnam War, his major domestic enemies were the protesters. As Ruth Gonchar and Dan Hahn wrote, "Nowhere is Nixon's isolation from the 'liberal community' more apparent than in his reactions to campus dissent. Clearly, students are outsiders. Years of distrust and isolation have desensitized Nixon to student voices."[13]

In the fall of 1969, even a president less paranoid than Richard Nixon might have been concerned about antiwar protest. After the chaos of the Democratic National Convention held in Chicago during August 1968, the movement seemed to many to be in disarray and out of public favor.[14] But antiwar activity had begun to pick up as 1969 passed its midpoint, and the Moratorium Day protest on October 15 was the "largest nationwide protest in American history."[15] In cities across the nation, thousands of people turned out to march, chant, hear speeches, and pass out literature. The demonstrations were generally nonviolent, thus avoiding the kind of negative press coverage that had attended the Chicago protests in 1968. Another, similar series of antiwar activities was planned for November, and leaders of the movement promised a recurrence each month until the war was ended.

Nixon was "angered and worried" by the mass demonstrations in October, and the "silent majority" speech was the first shot in his return salvo.[16] In dealing with antiwar protesters in the address, he committed an act of joining and an act of separation.

The joining involved an effort to combine, in the public's perception, the large number of moderate, peaceful opponents of the war with the radical, violent minority. He wanted the moderate Moratorium Committee to be seen as of the same stripe as the radical Weather Underground; the peaceful marchers would be lumped together with the bomb throwers.

It is difficult to say whether Nixon sincerely believed that all demonstrators were radical extremists or if he was cynically making the claim for his own purposes, but the truth was far removed from the president's depiction. The demonstrator-carried sign to which Nixon referred in his speech, "Lose in Vietnam, bring the boys home," may very well have existed, but the sentiment it expressed was not shared by all opponents of the war.[17] The spectrum of opinion concerning the proper ending of the conflict was quite broad, even among committed doves. Some groups and individuals wanted only a bombing halt and serious negotiations; others favored an announced timetable for withdrawal of U.S. forces; and some, like the demonstrator mentioned by Nixon, espoused a position expressed in the chant "Out Now!" As Campbell observed, "Only a small minority of the peace movement supported immediate, total withdrawal. The President's characterization of his opposition is designed to make the alternatives to Vietnamization appear as extreme as possible."[18]

As a result of this rhetorical act of joining, Nixon was able to engage in separation, or, more precisely, polarization. He tried to polarize his audience into two distinct groups: the noisy, violent dissidents who wanted an immediate, total termination of U.S. involvement in Vietnam and the "silent majority" of patriotic Americans who were willing to let the president pursue his plan for peace with honor. Some refer to this tactic as *antithesis*: uniting a group of people in the face of a common enemy, real or imagined.[19] It is more widely known, however, as *polarization*: splitting a population into two widely separated groups like the opposite poles of a magnet. As Andrew King and Floyd Douglas Anderson argue, "Polarization always exhibits two dimensions. On the one hand, it implies a powerful feeling of solidarity. . . . On the other hand, polarization also presupposes the existence of a perceived 'common foe' which the group must oppose."[20] In this way, antiwar protestors, regardless of their place in the spectrum of dissent, become "them" to the silent majority's "us." Any who disagree, in any public way, with the president's Vietnamization plan, are immediately classified as part of the howling, flag-burning mob at the gates.

THE TRIUMPHANT INDIVIDUAL

This cultural morality tale is, essentially, a hero myth. All cultures have their stories of heroism, of course, but this one is uniquely American. Only in the fabled "land of opportunity" is such accomplishment possible. The Triumphant Individual is the man or woman who works hard, sacrifices, overcomes obstacles, perseveres, and finally wins the prize—whether it is money, true love, an athletic contest, or a gunfight. In this mythology, the victory goes not to someone who started out with all the advantages but to "the humble guy who works hard, takes risks but has faith in himself and as a result eventually reaches or even exceeds his goals."[21] Such a person may well become a leader, and, as such, deserves to be admired, respected, and followed.

Clearly, Richard Nixon wished to portray himself in his "silent majority" speech as such a leader. First, he claims to deserve admiration and respect because he is telling the truth. It seems an accurate assessment to say that, for many Americans, to hear a president tell the truth in those days about Vietnam would be considered something of a novelty. As Hal Bochin argued, "Nixon based his persuasive appeals [in the November 3, 1969, speech] on principles and values [his audience] would readily accept. . . . The most important was truth, especially in light of the 'credibility gap' that had plagued the last years of the Johnson administration."[22]

But Nixon, in his self-depiction, is more than just a man who tells the truth. He is also a man who does what is right, regardless of the cost. After explaining his plan for Vietnamization, which involved a gradual reduction of U.S. combat forces on no fixed timetable, Nixon explains, "It is not the easy way. It is the right way. It is a plan which will end the war and serve the cause of peace—not just in Vietnam but in the Pacific and in the world."[23]

Nixon continually reminds his audience that, as commander-in-chief, the burden is his to bear, and the choices, all of them difficult, are his to make: "As President I hold the responsibility for choosing the best path to [a just and lasting peace] and then leading the Nation along it."[24] He thus belongs squarely within the tradition of the Triumphant Individual. He is virtuous, vigilant, and driven to follow the right course, no matter how difficult it may be. He does not shirk from his responsibility, which is to articulate and make into policy the will of the majority of Americans. Further, "Nixon sees himself as sole representative of the majority in all matters, and anyone who opposes him represents only a minority or extremist point of view."[25] Indeed, because Nixon was the leader of the majority, he portrayed himself as possessing all the virtues that the majority attributed to itself. He was, in his rhetoric, "the embodiment of all that was good and strong and God-fearing and right about the American people."[26] That his placement of himself in the niche reserved for national heroes was accepted, even if temporarily, was a great testament to the persuasive powers of the man who once had been known as "Tricky Dicky."

THE BENEVOLENT COMMUNITY

This cultural fable dates back to Puritan times, when the early New England communities were envisioned to function like "cities on a hill."

That is to say, they would serve as examples to the rest of the world of what a good and God-fearing people should be.[27] The meaning of benevolent community goes beyond the Puritans' fairly narrow religious perspective. In its broader, secular meaning, it refers to good people banding together to do good things. It is, in one sense, the Norman Rockwell view of America: small towns full of people who help each other organize charity drives and quilting bees. It can also function at the national level, when a nation is asked to buy war bonds or support the Great Society, or provide George Bush with his "thousand points of light." Importantly, the benevolence of the community is defined by action, not mere disposition. The group (or nation, or whatever) achieves the distinction of benevolence because of the virtuous acts it performs.

Although much of Nixon's telling of this morality tale in his speech is implicit, he does make some explicit references to benevolent community, as when he says, "We Americans are a do-it-yourself people. . . . Instead of teaching someone else to do a job, we like to do it ourselves."[28] Later in the speech he says, "Our greatness as a nation has been our capacity to do what had to be done when we knew our course was right."[29]

But most of Nixon's attempts to appeal to the myth of the benevolent community are implied from the subtext of the address. For example, the section of the speech that gives rise to its famous nickname is quite brief: "And so tonight—to you, the great silent majority of my fellow Americans—I ask for your support."[30] This is the only reference to the "silent majority" by name in the entire address. In light of the rest of the speech, however, it speaks volumes. It asks the middle-class viewers and listeners to distinguish themselves from the demonstrators who threaten to destroy America. It is Nixon's negative and falsely dichotomous depiction of his opponents that allowed his middle-class listeners to define themselves in a positive light. The demonstrators were loud and disruptive; the president's listeners were quiet and law-abiding. The young opponents of the war often seemed to flaunt traditional American values; the "silent majority" believed in those values. The protesters wanted immediate withdrawal of U.S. forces from Vietnam (or so Nixon had said); the loyal Americans would support the president's plan for Vietnamizing the war.

The members of the "silent majority" were not necessarily "hawks." Opinion polls showed that those who wanted to continue or even escalate the war were a definite minority by 1969.[31] Nixon's newly named constituency generally wanted the war to end but on terms that could somehow be construed as honorable. The members of the "silent majority" were conventionally patriotic, and they shared the anti-Communism characteristic that had long been an important value in American society.[32] They did not want, in the words of Nixon's archetypal protester, to "lose in Vietnam." They wanted to disengage while putting the best face on things. In addition, they disapproved greatly of the antiwar protesters. About a month after Nixon's speech, 59 percent of those surveyed considered themselves to be part of the "silent majority." Of that group, 74 percent defined the term as referring to people who believed that "protesters have gone too far."[33] Thus, this newly identified segment of the population was less prowar than it was anti-protest. It was a community that perceived itself as benevolent because Richard Nixon had said it was. Its members were patriotic, believers in "law and order," supporters of the president, and possessers of the traditional American values. They were benevolent toward all those whom they believed to be like themselves.

THE ROT AT THE TOP

The United States was founded in response to perceived abuses of power by the British government, and since then Americans have tended to be suspicious of the power-wielders in their own society. Although the observation that "all power tends to corrupt, and absolute power corrupts absolutely" was made by an Englishman, it accurately expresses the feeling behind Reich's fourth and last cultural myth. In application, this fable "has one of two targets—political corruption or economic exploitation."[34]

The myth is essentially an attack on elites. This may seem curious, since Richard Nixon was clearly in an elite position. Certainly, he did not wish to call down an attack on himself, but American society has multiple elites. Nixon may have been at the pinnacle of the political elite (or, at least, the executive branch thereof), but he often found himself in competition with other groups and institutions in the society. Two elite groups he particularly resented were academics, especially those from prestigious schools, such as ones in the Ivy League, and the news media.[35]

Nixon did not make overt reference to the "rot at the top" myth in his "silent majority" address, but the speech signaled the beginning of a concentrated rhetorical attack by the administration on some of its foes, especially students, professors, news commentators, and reporters. The point man in this campaign was Vice President Spiro T. Agnew. During the 1968 election campaign, Nixon had used Agnew as a political and rhetorical "enforcer," which he continued once in the White House. Agnew was given the task of talking tough and skewering the administration's enemies, thus allowing Nixon to remain aloof and "presidential."[36]

The first elite target was the national news media. After the "silent majority" speech, Nixon watched television political commentators dissect the address, and he was not pleased. Agnew received his orders, and, ten days later, delivered a blistering attack on the news editors, anchors, and commentators of the national television networks. That he was attacking them *as elites* becomes clear when one notices the repeated references to "a small group of men," "a handful of men," and a "small band." He also pointed out that "these commentators and producers live and work in the geographical and intellectual confines of Washington, D.C., or New York City."[37] Other speeches in a similar vein soon followed.

Nor were the colleges and universities spared Agnew's sharp tongue. Nixon's frustrations with antiwar college students and their professors was well known, although he rarely discussed them in public.[38] It is not known how much of this anger was due to the fact that much more protest activity took place at elite schools such as Columbia and Harvard than at lesser-known institutions. Agnew was talking about student protesters when he used the phrase "an effete corps of impudent snobs who consider themselves intellectuals." He also spoke out against the "radical faculty" on university campuses who were "poisoning the student mind against the validity of our system."[39] Clearly, all of this criticism seems consistent with the myth of "rot at the top," if one defines "top" somewhat loosely. Two of America's treasured institutions, journalism and education, were depicted as being in the hands of ideologues who were hostile to traditional values and to the administration who purported to represent them. These "snobs" thought they were better than everyone else, but Nixon, Agnew, and the newly emerging "silent majority" could see them for what they were.

The preceding discussion may clarify the widespread approbation that greeted Nixon's speech of November 3, 1969. It was, truly, a "rhetoric of shared values," as the president used fundamental cultural myths to show the members of his audience that he was their champion and hence deserving of their support in his struggle against the enemy in Vietnam and the enemy at home. Richard Nixon, the Triumphant Individual, placed himself directly in the gap that separated the howling mob from the benevolent community. There might be a few know-it-alls who would criticize his actions, but they would not, and should not, be heeded. The president would make the right decision, even when it was not "the easy thing to do."

NOTES

1. Robert P. Newman, "Under the Veneer: Nixon's Vietnam Speech of November 3, 1969," *Quarterly Journal of Speech* 56 (1970): 113–128.

2. Karlyn Kohrs Campbell, *Critiques of Contemporary Rhetoric* (Belmont, CA: Wadsworth Publishing, 1972), 50.

3. Forbes Hill, "Conventional Wisdom—Traditional Form: The President's Message of November 3, 1969," *Quarterly Journal of Speech* 58 (1972): 373–386.

4. Herman Stelzner, "The Quest Story and Nixon's November 3, 1969 Address," *Quarterly Journal of Speech* 57 (1971): 163–172.

5. John Morton Blum, *Years of Discord* (New York: W. W. Norton, 1991), 355. See also Charles DeBenedetti, *An American Ordeal* (Syracuse, NY: Syracuse University Press, 1990), 259.

6. Newman, 177.

7. Robert B. Reich, *Tales of a New America* (New York: Vintage Books, 1987), 6.

8. Ibid., 8–11.

9. Ibid., 8.

10. This discussion owes much to Charles U. Larson, *Persuasion: Reception and Responsibility*, 5th ed. (Belmont, CA: Wadsworth Publishing, 1989), 231–232.

11. Richard Nixon, "Address to the Nation on the War in Vietnam, November 3, 1969," in *Public Papers of the Presidents of the United States: Richard Nixon, 1969* (Washington, DC: Government Printing Office, 1970), p. 908.

12. Ibid., 909.

13. Ruth M. Gonchar and Dan F. Hahn, "Richard Nixon and Presidential Mythology," *Journal of Applied Communications Research* 1 (1973): 28.

14. David W. Levy, *The Debate Over Vietnam* (Baltimore: Johns Hopkins University Press, 1991), 153.

15. William E. Jurma, "Moderate Movement Leadership and the Vietnam Moratorium Committee," *Quarterly Journal of Speech* 68 (1982): 265.

16. Melvin Small, *Johnson, Nixon, and the Doves* (New Brunswick, NJ: Rutgers University Press, 1988), 187.

17. Newman, 172.

18. Campbell, 51. See also Theodore Otto Windt, Jr., *Presidents and Protesters: Political Rhetoric in the 1960s* (Tuscaloosa, AL: University of Alabama Press, 1990), 122.

19. Phillip K. Tompkins, *Communication as Action* (Belmont, CA: Wadsworth Publishing, 1982), 47–48.

20. Andrew A. King and Floyd Douglas Anderson, "Nixon, Agnew, and the 'Silent Majority': A Case Study in the Rhetoric of Polarization," *Western Speech* 35 (1971): 244.

21. Larson, 232.

22. Hal W. Bochin, *Richard Nixon: Rhetorical Strategist* (Westport, CT: Greenwood Press, 1990), 58.

23. Nixon, 907–908.

24. Ibid., 909.

25. Windt, p. 128.

26. Stephen E. Ambrose, *Nixon: The Triumph of a Politician, 1962–1972* (New York: Simon and Schuster, 1989), 412.

27. Reich, 10.

28. Nixon, 905.

29. Ibid., 908.

30. Ibid., 909.

31. Murray Edelman, *Political Language* (New York: Academic Press, 1977), 30.

32. Milton J. Rosenberg, Sidney Verba, Philip E. Converse, *Vietnam and the Silent Majority: The Dove's Guide* (New York: Harper & Row, 1970), 42–43.

33. DeBenedetti, 266.

34. Larson, 234.

35. Gonchar and Hahn, 27–28.

36. Newman, 177.

37. "Vice President Agnew on Televised News," in Carroll C. Arnold, *Criticism of Oral Rhetoric* (Columbus, OH: Charles E. Merrill, 1974), 367–375. This is generally regarded as the most accurate of the published versions of the speech.

38. Small, 188.

39. Cited in King and Anderson, 247, 249.

Part Two

Antiwar Rhetoric

Chapter Five

Daniel Berrigan and the Rhetoric of Ultra-Resistance

This chapter examines the role of the Reverend Daniel Berrigan, Catholic priest and antiwar activist, in the Catholic Ultra-Resistance movement and discusses the specific rhetorical strategies in Berrigan's rhetoric concerning the Vietnam War.

The term "Ultra-Resistance," coined by writer Francine du Plessix Gray in 1970, refers to a loosely knit group of Catholic radicals who through civil disobedience opposed the U.S. government's policies in Vietnam. The most common form of that civil disobedience was the destruction of war-related property, usually draft files.[1] The phrase has often been used synonomously with "Catholic Left," although it may be argued that there were some American Catholics who actively opposed the war in Vietnam but who eschewed civil disobedience as a protest tactic. "Ultra-Resistance" is thus a more precise term than "Catholic Left." Although fairly small in numbers—some estimates place the number of activists as low as two hundred[2]—the Ultra-Resistance nonetheless was rhetorically important. Charles Wilkinson concluded that "the Catholic Anti-War movement in the United States . . . during the Vietnam war achieved a level of significance far beyond itself, particularly its size."[3] That significance was such that several commentators on the movement's historical context place it "at the vanguard of antiwar protest" during the Vietnam era.[4]

The Berrigan brothers, Daniel and Philip, both Catholic priests, were in the forefront of the particular type of civil disobedience that characterized the Ultra-Resistance. Philip led the first draft board raid, in Baltimore, in October 1967. He also instigated the "Catonsville Nine" action of May 1968. In the latter, he was accompanied by Daniel, who wrote the press release explaining the burning of draft files with napalm that occurred there. The impact of the Berrigans on the movement has been characterized as equivalent to a *sine qua non*:

Philip and Daniel Berrigan, both priests, were undoubtedly the most noteworthy figures in the movement; so significant that a reading of the history and literature of the movement quickly leads one to the conclusion that without them the movement would not have been more than a slowly developing trend in American Catholic thought and letters.[5]

Because this description applied to both Berrigan brothers, the reader may legitimately wonder why this chapter focuses only on Daniel. The reason is that, by and large, the two brothers gravitated toward different kinds of activities, and Daniel's activities are of much greater relevance to the rhetorical critic. As journalist Garry Wills wrote, "The uneducated public thinks in terms of 'the Berrigans' as if they were twins, interchangeable, a two-man act, while in fact they could not be more different."[6] The distinction, and its relevance for the student of rhetoric, is made clear by Patricia McNeal:

The idea for the destruction of draft files and the organization of similar actions which would occur after Catonsville were mainly the work of Philip Berrigan. He was the organizer of Catonsville and, as a peace activist, he was there. But Philip remained in the background. It was his brother, Daniel, who emerged as a spokesman for the group and who provided the rationale for such actions.[7]

It is possible to deduce Daniel Berrigan's preeminence in the movement through the work of outside commentators, such as McNeal. One can come to the same conclusion, however, by examining the way that Daniel Berrigan was perceived by members of the Catholic Ultra-Resistance. As a writer for *Newsweek* pointed out in the magazine's issue of April 20, 1972, "It is Dan, the poet and celebrated 'holy outlaw,' who has become the rallying point for the Catholic Left."[8] The same article provides relevant testimony from a member of the movement:

"One of the reasons Dan appealed to us," says Linda Finlay, a professor of philosophy at Ithaca College, "was that all the abstractions of morality and religion were given a new life. Whatever idealism we had left over from our Catholic education was suddenly made meaningful by what he had to say and by what he did."[9]

Thus, Daniel Berrigan's rhetoric was of considerable significance during the Vietnam War and helped to inspire people to protest that war in dramatic ways. Although the symbolic value of the Catonsville incident has been the subject of scholarly examination,[10] a detailed study of Berrigan's rhetoric has not yet been provided.

A BIOGRAPHICAL SKETCH

Daniel Berrigan was born on May 9, 1921, in Virginia, Minnesota. A year later, the family moved to Syracuse, New York, after Berrigan's father lost his railroad job due to his involvement in the Socialist Party.[11] The elder Berrigan was a strong supporter of trade unionism and a lapsed Catholic. His wife, Frida Fromhart Berrigan, was a German immigrant and a devout Catholic. That her views on religion prevailed over her husband's is evident when one considers that the family sent three of its sons into the priesthood. Years later, when Daniel and Philip were standing trial for their antiwar activities, they cited their mother's influence as being important in their decisions to defy the government.[12]

Daniel felt the call to the priesthood from his youth, and in 1939, at the age of eighteen, he was accepted for study in the Society of Jesus, known more familiarly as the Jesuits. Daniel's rationale for choosing that religious order, which at the time required a thirteen-year training period before ordination, seems characteristic of him:

When I was sixteen a friend and I wrote in for literature from all the orders in the United States we could think of—Benedictines, Augustinians, Dominicans— about forty of them. What impressed us about the Jesuits was that they didn't seem to want us. All the other orders were trying to rope us in by showing us photographs of jazzy swimming pools in their prospectus. But the Jebbies just had a couple of tight little quotes from St. Ignatius in a very stark pamphlet. We thought that cool scene was revolutionary. We applied immediately.[13]

Daniel was ordained a priest by the Society of Jesus in 1951. His early duties included serving as a chaplain to U.S. forces in Germany and teaching in a Jesuit preparatory school in Brooklyn. He served on the faculty of a Jesuit college, LeMoyne, in Syracuse, from 1957 to 1963, and there he first began to encounter young people who were involved in the civil rights struggle and in pacifism.[14]

As the Vietnam War began to impinge on American consciousness in the mid–1960s, Daniel Berrigan's concern—and opposition—grew. In 1965, he was back in New York City, this time as editor of *Jesuit Missions*, a liberal Catholic magazine. Between editorial duties, he became involved in fasts, public prayer, and sit-ins to protest against the war. In time, his peace activities came to the attention of Francis Cardinal Spellman, head of the Archdiocese of New York and a strong supporter of the war. Although, strictly speaking, religious orders such as the Jesuits are responsible only to the Vatican, Spellman put enough pressure on

Berrigan's local superiors to have him sent on an extended trip to Mexico and South America.[15] Berrigan was learning that opposition to the war would not be without its costs.

During his "exile" to South America, Berrigan saw poverty more severe than he had ever experienced, even during the Depression, and he quickly concluded that the poor were kept that way by the alliance of powerful business interests and the politicians who served them. The trip radicalized him further. As one of his biographers has written, "Sending Daniel Berrigan to Latin America was like tossing Br'er Rabbit into the briar patch."[16]

Exile was short-lived, however. In New York, friends, coworkers and admirers exerted some pressure of their own, and through marches, full-page ads in the *New York Times*, and other protests, secured Berrigan's return after only three months.[17] Back in the United States, he began heading toward even more direct confrontations with authority. As Berrigan himself states, "I began after my return to the States in the autumn of 1964, as loudly as I could, to say 'no' to the war."[18] One facet of his opposition was the founding of Clergy Concerned about Vietnam, an organization that later became Clergy and Laity Concerned about Vietnam.[19] In 1967, he was invited to Cornell University as a chaplain, and his opposition to the war became so widely known that the following year he and Boston University professor Howard Zinn were invited by the government of North Vietnam to visit that country to escort home some captured American pilots who were being released as a goodwill gesture. Berrigan's experiences in Hanoi, including sitting through an American air raid, strengthened, if that were possible, his already strong belief that the war was wrong and needed to be halted.[20]

During the same year, Daniel's brother, Philip, also a priest and antiwar activist, and three friends had poured blood on draft files in Baltimore as a symbol of protest. In 1968, while out on bail pending appeal, Philip came to his brother with an idea for another, more significant protest action. Daniel writes of his reaction:

I was at the time very far from their understanding of things. But I was shaken into reflectiveness. I had gone to Hanoi, I had experienced American bombings and brought home prisoners of war. So when Philip approached me in early May with a new action into which I was urgently invited, my immediate reaction was one of bewildered sympathy and shaken readiness. I was faced with the evidence of intransigent courage on the part of those who were already in legal trouble up to their very necks. Imagine Philip and Tom Lewis [a member of the Baltimore Four, and later, of the Catonsville Nine], men already under threat of several years of imprisonment, calmly repeating the same action that had brought them into jeopardy!

Like a shipwreck or a man sucked into quicksand or a drowning man, to whom almost every resource of friendship and ingenuity is lacking, and yet who somehow emerges alive, I say simply that I was saved at the last moment.[21]

The action proposed by Philip to his brother was another draft board raid, this one in the small Baltimore suburb of Catonsville. What occurred there, in May 1968, has already been described. Of the significance of that act, McNeal has written:

For Catholic peace activists, Catonsville signaled a dramatic move to the left in their resistance to war.... Soon after Catonsville similar draft board actions occurred in Milwaukee and Chicago.... Participants of draft action became known in the press as members of the "Catholic Left" or the "Catholic Resistance."[22]

Thus, in a very real sense, the action at Catonsville was the impetus to the movement that became known as the Catholic Ultra-Resistance.

THE NATURE OF RHETORICAL STRATEGIES

A strategy is a choice made with a view toward securing a particular effect. A "rhetorical strategy" is thus a choice among symbols designed to secure a particular effect on an audience. As Karlyn Kohrs Campbell puts it, "The description of strategies determines how the rhetorician shapes his material in terms of his audience and his purposes."[23] Such choices are called "symbolic strategies" by some scholars.[24] Rhetorical strategies involve "language techniques that alter verbal behavior" on the part of the rhetor,[25] as well as a "conscious or unconscious response to a problem, question or situation."[26]

Rhetorical strategies may involve more than the choice of language for spoken discourse. Such strategies include any sort of behavior, verbal or nonverbal, that has symbolic significance for the rhetor and his or her audience, including protest marches, meetings, posters, and the destruction of property.[27] In James Chesebro's terms, a rhetorical strategy may be properly seen as "any act which conveys a message to others."[28]

A number of scholars have used rhetorical strategy as a perspective from which to examine various types of discourse,[29] including recent radical movements in the United States.[30] It therefore seems a useful perspective from which to view the symbolic choices made by Daniel Berrigan, who was a major force behind a recent American radical movement.

BERRIGAN'S RHETORICAL STRATEGIES

The four specimens of Berrigan's rhetoric analyzed here were chosen because they are the most widely circulated of his writings from this

period and are thus the most likely to have been read by other members
of the movement, as well as by the general public. They are the following:

—"The Catonsville Statement," given to reporters at the time of the Catonsville
  Nine action, printed in several newspapers, and reprinted in a publication of
  the Catonsville Nine Defense Committee, *Delivered into Resistance*[31];

—"A Meditation from Catonsville," written by Daniel Berrigan during the week
  before the Catonsville action and released after the action was completed. It
  was reprinted in several newspapers, in *Delivered into Resistance*, and as a
  preface to Berrigan's book, *Night Flight to Hanoi*[32];

—"How to Make a Difference," which appeared in the magazine *Commonweal*
  in 1971.[33]

—"Letter to the Weathermen," which appeared in *The Village Voice* in 1970.[34]

The latter two pieces were written and published while Berrigan was
a fugitive from justice, following his conviction on charges stemming
from the Catonsville raid.

Analysis of these writings shows the presence of five consistently
recurring rhetorical strategies: support for nonviolence as a protest tactic,
a call for others to resist, disdain for the government, disdain for corporations, and religious references.

One of the strategies found consistently in Daniel Berrigan's antiwar
essays was support for nonviolence as a technique for protesting the
war. Berrigan's entire rationale for acting against the war in Vietnam
was that he perceived it as wasteful of human life. The use of violence
to protest this other violence was, to him, anathema. In "Meditation
from Catonsville," he maintains that "killing is disorder, life and gentle-
ness and community and unselfishness is the only order we recognize."[35]
He writes in the same piece, "We have chosen to say, with the gift of
our liberty, if necessary with our lives; the violence stops here, the death
stops here."[36]

In "How to Make a Difference," Berrigan writes of his commitment
to continue with "illegal non-violent actions."[37]

In his letter to the Weathermen, Berrigan expresses to this avowedly
violent group the belief that "affection and compassion and nonviolence
are now common resources once more."[38] He then admonishes the
Weathermen that "we are to strive to become such men and women as
may, in a new world, be nonviolent."[39]

A second strategy in Berrigan's rhetoric was a call for others to resist
the war. In "Meditation from Catonsville," Berrigan asks his audience
a series of questions, the hortatory implications of which seem clear:

We ask our fellow Christians to consider in their hearts a question which has
tortured us, night and day, since the war began. How many must die before

our voices are heard, how many must be tortured, dislocated, starved, maddened? How long must the world's resources be raped in the service of legalized murder? When, at what point, will you say no to this war?[40]

Later in this meditation, Berrigan encourages resistance among his audience by describing the rewards that, he believes, will accrue to those who resist:

In a time of death, some men—the resisters, those who work hardily for social change, those who preach and embrace the unpalatable truth—such men overcome death, their lives are bathed in the light of the resurrection, the truth has set them free.[41]

In "How to Make a Difference," Berrigan depicts resistance as growing gradually and being based on example. It may have been this belief that prompted him to act to set himself up as an example, even at the price of a jail sentence:

What we seek, acting cooly, politically, out of the truth of our lives and tradition is to pull the mask of legitimacy from the inhuman and blind face of power. We seek at the same time, to open the eyes of more and more of our friends, to bring a larger community of resistance into being. . . . Even if a few men say no, courageously, constantly, clearsightedly, more men will be drawn to say no; fewer men likewise will continue to say yes.[42]

In "Letter to the Weathermen," Berrigan encourages the members of the Weather Underground to continue down the path of resistance that they have chosen:

Some of your actions are going to involve inciting and conflicting and trashing, and these actions are very difficult for thoughtful people. But I came upon a rule of thumb somewhere which might be of some help to us; do only what one cannot not do.[43]

A third rhetorical strategy is disdain for the U.S. government. Berrigan saw himself and the government at opposite poles of a continuum, with the government representing death, destruction, and a flagrant lack of concern for the helpless, and with him standing for life, love, and a concern for the downtrodden, prompted by Christ's gospel. Two very clear examples of this disdain are found in the "Catonsville Statement": "The rulers of America want their global wars fought as cheaply as possible."[44] Later in the same press release, he seems to be giving voice to some indignation when he adds, "We are appalled by the ruse of the American ruling class invoking the cry for 'Law and Order' to mask and perpetuate injustice."[45]

In "Meditation from Catonsville," Berrigan combines a religious reference, another recurring element, with disdain for the government when, in reference to Christ, he says, "He sets up the cross and dies on it; in the Rose Garden of the executive mansion, on the D.C. mall, in the courtyard of the Pentagon."[46] In the same essay, Berrigan maintains that the government "is announcing ever more massive paramilitary means to confront the disorder in the cities."[47]

In "How to Make a Difference," Berrigan expresses his cynical view of politicians by saying, "Philip and I have never been able simply to stand around wringing our hands at the latest outrage of Nixon or Johnson or their myrmidons."[48] He also attacks the U.S. government by comparing it to other regimes, all repressive. He claims that the treatment of his brother, Philip, in prison

is a ratio of punishment to crime which recalls the Nazi or Fascist treatment of hostages of the maquis, the South African or Angolan disposition of captured guerrillas, the Ky bullies moving against Buddhists and students, the U.S. incarceration of Panthers without bail.[49]

Another strategy found in Berrigan's rhetoric is "disdain for corporations." This might be seen as an offshoot of his disdain for the government, since he saw American government and capitalism as inextricably linked for their exploitative purposes. This is illustrated when he writes that "U.S. foreign profits run substantially higher than domestic profits so industry flees abroad under government patronage and the protection of the CIA, military counter insurgency and conflict-management teams."[50]

Berrigan tells the Weathermen that "I have a great fear of American violence, not only out there in the military and diplomacy, but in economics, in industry and advertising."[51]

The final strategy found in Berrigan's rhetoric I call "religious references." It is not surprising that this element is present. He is a Jesuit priest, and his motivation for protest, whether of the Catholic Church's support of repressive governments in Latin America, the Vietnam War, or the manufacture of nuclear weapons, has always been fundamentally religious. He believes he is obligated by the message of the Gospel to defy the state, much as did the early Christians during the time of the Roman Empire. In "Meditation from Catonsville," Berrigan writes that his motivation for engaging in the draft board raid came from

thinking of that other Child, of Whom the poet Luke speaks. The infant was taken up in the arms of an old man, whose tongue grew resonant and vatic at the touch of that beauty. And the old man spoke; this child is set for the fall and rise of many in Israel, a sign that is spoken against.[52]

In the "Catonsville Statement," Berrigan describes the Catonsville Nine, as the group who raided the Catonsville draft board became known, as "Catholic Christians who take the gospel of our Faith seriously."[53] And in his letter to the Weathermen, he writes, "as they say about Jesus, some people, even to this day, he gave us hope."[54]

The question may legitimately be raised as to whether Daniel Berrigan's rhetoric had any measurable impact. The best answer seems to be this: he had an effect, but an indirect one. As I have argued both here and elsewhere,[55] he had a significant influence on the actions and the rhetoric of the Catholic Ultra-Resistance, and the Ultra-Resistance had some effects on the struggle against the war.

One result of the actions of the Ultra-Resistance may be seen in terms of the support engendered among nonresisters. Many people who did not choose to put their freedom in jeopardy by committing felonious acts were nonetheless influenced by the protest actions of the Ultra-Resistance. Each trial of draft board raiders or corporate disruptors produced "festivals of support" for which supporters staged marches and rallies outside the jails and courthouses containing the accused.[56] As Gordon Zahn noted, "It is a conservative estimate to say that tens of thousands were reached" in this manner "and many of these were undoubtedly moved to more direct opposition to the war."[57]

Another effect involved the Selective Service System. As Charles Meconis argued, "The Catholic Left's campaign against the Selective Service System must be included in any attempt to assess the impact of the movement's activities."[58] Although the Ultra-Resistance cannot be credited with achieving its goal of making the draft grind to a halt, it can be said to have inhibited its functioning. This has been attested to by two members of President Ford's Vietnam War Clemency Board, who concluded:

The activities of . . . the Berrigans and the others failed to produce 100,000 signatures on Resistance petitions, and they did not bring the war machine to a halt. But they did draw public attention to draft resistance, and heavy media exposure contributed to the grass-roots, unorganized movement by more than a half-million young men who broke the law and defied their draft boards. Enormous numbers of draft-age men were refusing induction, forcing local boards to refer their cases to federal prosecutors. The courts may not have been jammed, but the prosecutor's offices were. The draft did not collapse, but it did lose much of its ability to enforce induction orders.[59]

The Rev. Daniel Berrigan is not a man given to moderation or compromise on what he regards as moral issues. During the Vietnam War, he deliberately made himself an outcast in his own country and within his own church, standing foursquare against his government's prosecution of the war. Just as the Weathermen became outlaws in response to their reading of Marx, Lenin, Mao, Che Guevara, and Franz Fanon, so too did Daniel Berrigan embrace the roles of felon, fugitive, and federal prisoner because of his understanding of the Gospel message. His actions were inseparable from his religious faith, and so was his rhetoric.

NOTES

1. Francine du Plessix Gray, "The Ultra-Resistance," *Trials of the Resistance*, ed. New York Review of Books (New York: New York Review Press, 1970), 128.

2. Charles A. Meconis, *With Clumsy Grace: The American Catholic Left 1961–1975* (New York: The Seabury Press, 1979), 149.

3. Charles A. Wilkinson, "A Rhetorical Definition of Movements," *Central States Speech Journal* 27 (Summer 1976): 92.

4. William O'Rourke, *The Harrisburg 7 and the New Catholic Left* (New York: Thomas Y. Crowell, 1972), 157.

5. Charles A. Wilkinson, "The Rhetoric of Movements: Definition and Methodological Approach, Applied to the Catholic Anti-War Movement in the United States" (Ph.D. dissertation, Northwestern University, 1975), 104.

6. Garry Wills, "Love on Trial," *Harper's*, July 1972, 64.

7. Patricia F. McNeal, "The American Catholic Peace Movement 1928–1972" (Ph.D. dissertation, Temple University, 1974), 242–243.

8. "Where's the Catholic Left?" *Newsweek*, April 10, 1972, 68.

9. Ibid.

10. John H. Patton, "Rhetoric at Catonsville: Daniel Berrigan, Conscience and Image Alteration," *Today's Speech* 23 (Winter, 1975): 3–12.

11. Thomas Harrison, "Daniel Berrigan," in *Political Profiles: The Johnson Years*, ed. Nelson Lichtenstein (New York: Facts on File), 41.

12. Anne Klejment, *The Berrigans: A Bibliography of Published Works by Daniel, Philip and Elizabeth McAlister Berrigan* (New York: Garland Publishing, 1979), xvii.

13. Francine du Plessix Gray, *Divine Disobedience* (New York: Alfred A. Knopf, 1970), 64–65.

14. Harrison, 42.

15. Ibid.

16. Richard Curtis, *The Berrigan Brothers* (New York: Hawthorn Books, 1974), 58–59.

17. Ibid., 55–63.

18. Daniel Berrigan, *No Bars to Manhood* (New York: Bantam Books, 1971), 10.

19. Herbert M. Levine, "Daniel Berrigan," in *Political Profiles: The Nixon/Ford Years*, ed. Eleonora W. Schoenbaum (New York: Facts on File, 1979), 48–49.

20. Berrigan's report of his trip to North Vietnam, along with his reactions to it, are published in Daniel Berrigan, *Night Flight to Hanoi: War Diary with Eleven Poems* (New York: Macmillan, 1968).

21. Berrigan, *No Bars to Manhood*, 14–15.

22. McNeal, 241 and 272.

23. Karlyn Kohrs Campbell, *Critiques of Contemporary Rhetoric* (Belmont, CA: Wadsworth Publishing, 1972), 18.

DANIEL BERRIGAN AND ULTRA-RESISTANCE 77

24. See, for example, James L. Golden, Goodwin F. Berquist, and William E. Coleman, *The Rhetoric of Western Thought* (Dubuque, IA: Kendall/Hunt Publishing, 1976), 243.
25. Campbell, 36.
26. James W. Chesebro, "Rhetorical Strategies of the Radical Revolutionary," *Today's Speech* 20 (1972): 45.
27. Ibid., 47. See also the editor's introduction in Haig A. Bosmajian, ed., *Dissent: Symbolic Behavior and Rhetorical Strategies* (Boston: Allyn and Bacon, 1972), 1–11.
28. Chesebro, 47.
29. Duane A. Litfin, "Muskie's 'Five Smooth Stones': An Analysis of Rhetorical Strategies and Tactics in His 1970 Election-Eve Speech," *Central States Speech Journal* 23 (1972): 5–10; J. J. Makay, "The Rhetorical Strategies of Governor George Wallace in the 1964 Maryland Primary," *Southern Speech Journal* 36 (1970): 164–175; Herbert W. Simons, "Requirements, Problems and Strategies: A Theory of Persuasion for Social Movements," *Quarterly Journal of Speech* 61 (1970): 1–11; and Arthur Smith, *Rhetoric of Black Revolution* (Boston: Allyn and Bacon, 1969), especially Chapter 1.
30. See Chesebro, 44–52.
31. Reprinted in Sarah A. Fahy, "The Catonsville Nine Action: A Study of an American Catholic Resistance Position" (Ph.D. dissertation, Temple University, 1975), 203–207.
32. Reprinted in Fahy, 211–214.
33. Daniel Berrigan, "How to Make a Difference," *Commonweal*, August 7, 1970, 384–386.
34. Daniel Berrigan, "Letter to the Weathermen," in *The Eloquence of Protest*, ed. Harrison G. Salisbury (Boston: Houghton Mifflin, 1972), 13–18.
35. "Meditation from Catonsville," 213.
36. Ibid.
37. "How to Make a Difference," 386.
38. "Letter to the Weathermen," 15.
39. Ibid., 17.
40. "Meditation from Catonsville," 213.
41. Ibid., 214.
42. "How to Make a Difference," 386.
43. "Letter to the Weathermen," 16.
44. "Catonsville Statement," 203.
45. Ibid., 207.
46. "Meditation from Catonsville," 212.
47. Ibid.
48. "How to Make a Difference," 386.
49. Ibid., 384.
50. "Catonsville Statement," 204.
51. "Letter to the Weathermen," 17.
52. "Meditation from Catonsville," 212.
53. "Catonsville Statement," 205.
54. "Letter to the Weathermen," 15.
55. J. Justin Gustainis, "Daniel Berrigan and the Catholic Ultra-Resistance:

The Roots of a Rhetorical Genre" (Ph.D. dissertation, Bowling Green State University, 1981).

56. Gordon Zahn, "The Berrigans—A Catholic Pacifist's View," *Dissent* 18 (1971): 201.

57. Zahn, 201.

58. Meconis, 151.

59. Lawrence M. Baskir and William A. Strauss, *Chance and Circumstance: The Draft, the War and the Vietnam Generation* (New York: Vintage Books, 1978), 67.

Chapter Six

The Rhetoric of Paradox: SDS and *The Port Huron Statement*

Any discussion of American opposition to the war in Vietnam requires consideration of the Students for a Democratic Society, more familiarly known as SDS. As Anthony Obershall wrote, "SDS was the largest pacesetting social movement organization of the middle and late Sixties. During its brief and stormy career . . . it pioneered or latched on to the central issues and activities of The Movement."[1] The history of SDS, according to Frederick Miller, "encompasses most aspects of New Left organization, ideology, and tactics."[2]

During the decade of the 1960s, SDS experienced a number of changes in philosophy, leadership, and rhetoric, all of which culminated in the 1969 schism that destroyed the organization and gave rise to the Weathermen (see Chapter 7). But the early years of SDS saw great enthusiasm and activity among young Leftists in this country, largely due to the success of a rhetorical artifact that became known as *The Port Huron Statement*.

SDS had its first incarnation in the 1950s, as the Student League for Industrial Democracy—a kind of youth auxiliary of the socialist League for Industrial Democracy. The name was changed to Students for a Democratic Society in 1960, but the new title did little to attract interest among American college students; membership was small, a few hundred, at best, and only a handful of campuses hosted SLID chapters. That moribund state of affairs changed in 1962, however, following the first SDS national convention. At this meeting held in Port Huron, Michigan, a document was finalized, discussed, and adopted as the formal expression of the organization's philosophy. That document, which became known as *The Port Huron Statement*, was largely the work of Tom

Hayden, a University of Michigan student who would become SDS's next president.

Hayden's brainchild has been called "one of the most important political writings of the decade,"[3] "the manifesto for the emerging New Student Left,"[4] and "a moral critique of American society . . . a compelling vision of a regenerated society, and a sketch of a strategy for moving forward."[5] Kirkpatrick Sale, author of the most comprehensive history of SDS to date, argues that the significance of *The Port Huron Statement* as rhetoric is that "it gave to those dissatisfied with their nation an analysis by which to dissect it, to those pressing instinctively for change a vision of what to work for, to those feeling within themselves the need to act a strategy by which to become effective. No ideology can do more."[6]

Copies of the document were distributed to a number of student groups, and soon clamors for more copies poured into the SDS national office in New York City. Between 1962 and 1966, more than sixty thousand copies were printed and distributed.[7] The response among young Leftists was immediate and enthusiastic. *The Port Huron Statement* served, in Theodore Otto Windt's words, as a "clarion call" to young people across the land who were dissatisfied with the direction in which their country appeared to be headed.[8] Interest in SDS began to develop on many campuses, new chapters were opened, and membership increased—slowly at first, then by almost quantum leaps.

This chapter is an effort of explain why *The Port Huron Statement* struck such a responsive chord in so many idealistic young people. I argue that the document's wide popularity among student activists was due, at least in part, to the fact that it was grounded in paradox.

A paradox is a concept "containing at once features which, though contradictory, coexist."[9] It is, in other words, a way of linking two ideas that appear to be opposites. The deliberate construction of a paradox is thus, in Chesebro's words, an act that "creates and mediates relationships among diverse stimuli, attitudes, beliefs, and actions within a perceptual field."[10] Paradox takes mutually exclusive ideas and holds them together in dynamic tension.

A firm grasp of the notion of paradox is useful in understanding the rhetoric of *The Port Huron Statement*. Tom Hayden and the others involved in creating the document began by castigating several paradoxes that they perceived as endemic in American culture. The SDS assessment of the state of America in 1962 included the following:

We began to see complicated and disturbing paradoxes in our surrounding America. The declaration "all men are created equal . . . " rang hollow before the facts of Negro life in the South and the big cities of the North. The proclaimed peaceful intentions of the United States contradicted its economic and military investments in the Cold War status quo. . . .

With nuclear energy whole cities can easily be powered, yet the dominant nation-states seem more likely to unleash destruction greater than that incurred in all wars of human history. Although our own technology is destroying old and creating new forms of social organization, men still tolerate meaningless work and idleness. While two-thirds of mankind suffers undernourishment, our own upper classes revel amidst superfluous abundance.[11]

The *Statement* went on to discuss other apparent paradoxes: the continually increasing growth in world population was contrasted with the chaos that seemed to govern much of international relations; the desperate need for world leadership was compared unfavorably with America's stagnant policies and unclear direction; and, perhaps most importantly, the urgent need for change perceived by the young founders of SDS was juxtaposed with the larger society, which seemed to be saying that significant change was impossible.[12]

Although the authors of *The Port Huron Statement* used paradox as a vehicle for their critique of American society, their solutions to the problems discussed leaned heavily toward the paradoxical, as well. These responses included an apparent endorsement of secular religion, opposition to anti-Communism combined with criticism of the Soviet Union, an attack on elites that also called on an elite group to act as change agent, and the *Statement's* paradoxical view of universities.

This discussion begins with the paradox of secular religion. Milton Viorst once wrote, with what he probably regarded as a degree of irony, that "SDS was in far greater measure a religion than a bureaucracy, and the 'Port Huron Statement' became its scripture."[13] Viorst may have been more correct than he knew; I argue that *The Port Huron Statement* did, in fact, identify the principles for what might be considered a secular religion. By this term, which is a deliberate oxymoron, itself a type of paradox, I mean that the document expresses values that are entirely consistent with the Judeo-Christian religious tradition but without once making any reference to the divine being that Jews and Christians acknowledge as the source of those values. An examination of the *Statement's* depictions of human beings, their relationships with each other, and the nature, both actual and ideal, of their institutions makes this clear.

Writing in the days before concern over sexism in language had become widespread, the authors of *The Port Huron Statement* referred consistently to all human beings as men whom they described as "infinitely precious and possessed of unfulfilled capacities for reason, freedom, and love."[14] Men are also said to possess "unrealized potential for self-cultivation, self-direction, self-understanding, and creativity."[15] This is not a secular view of humanity, even though no divine source for these values is acknowledged. The perspective expressed may be similar to that of Emerson, the transcendentalist, who saw God in all living things.[16] Such a perspective may not be religious in the traditional sense, but it is a religious perspective nonetheless.

A similar conception pervades the *Statement's* discussion of human interaction. Hayden and his associates argued that "relationships should involve fraternity and honesty. . . . Human brotherhood must be willed . . . as a condition of future survival."[17] Further, human brotherhood was seen as being impeded by materialism. The alienation that many modern people experience from each other, the *Statement* claimed, would be overcome "only when a love of man overcomes the idolatrous worship of things."[18] Such asceticism would be recognized by monks anywhere, whether Benedictine or Buddhist. Ascetic philosophy is rarely seen in a secular context; it almost always has a religious motivation, although *The Port Huron Statement* never admits to any such impetus.

The view of human institutions in the document also seems evocative of religion. The indictment of existing institutions has a strongly moral basis. The social power structure is portrayed as relying on power "rooted in possession, privilege, or circumstance."[19] It is urged that such power be replaced by "uniqueness rooted in love, reflectiveness, reason and creativity."[20] The same is held to be true of political institutions. Existing governmental relationships, the document claims, have led to mindless conflict, and "[p]ast senselessness permits present brutality; present brutality is prelude to future deeds of still greater inhumanity."[21] In response, the authors advocate that the essential creativity of this nation "should be creating a world where hunger, poverty, disease, ignorance, violence, and exploitation are replaced as central features by abundance, reason, love, and international cooperation."[22] These are the same sentiments often expressed today in televised public service announcements sponsored by any one of several religious organizations. They are essentially religious preachings, but without the acknowledgement of a divine being. Thus, *The Port Huron Statement* contains what Alan Adelson has described as "an almost religious description of how life should be."[23] The view is almost religious, but it does not invoke the deity. As such, it is a prime example of paradox.

Another manifestation of paradoxical argument in the document involves anti-Communism and the Soviet Union. Perhaps the boldest (for 1962) ideas in the *Statement* were those repudiating anti-Communism as a working philosophy for American life.[24] Senator Joseph McCarthy was not long in his grave, and his spectre still haunted much of the political landscape. It was this legacy that Hayden and the others were reacting against.[25] *The Port Huron Statement* contended that anti-Communism had become a "major social problem for those who want to construct a more democratic America."[26] Anti-Communism, it was argued, perverted the idealism of those who wished to serve their country in a meaningful way.[27] Further, it provided a ready platform for those of the far political right who wanted to justify their fascistic leanings.[28] Finally, the *Statement* alleged that anti-Communism was frequently used as a pretext by America's leaders to justify a wide range of militaristic policies and to stifle constructive debate about those policies.[29]

That said, the document was clearly not a paean to Communism or Communist governments. Indeed, the Soviet Union came in for considerable criticism. "As democrats," the *Statement's* authors said, "we are in basic opposition to the Communist system."[30] The Soviets were castigated for their "total suppression of organized opposition,"[31] their willingness to sacrifice human life in the furtherance of their political goals, their confusion of socialism with bureaucracy, and the undemocratic nature of their political system.[32] Communism, said Hayden and his associates, "has failed, in every sense, to achieve its stated intention of leading a worldwide movement for human emancipation."[33]

Thus, the argument was that American anti-Communism was clearly undesirable, but that Soviet Communism was eminently worthy of criticism. The essentially paradoxical viewpoint thus exhibited seems clear and is equally apparent when *The Port Huron Statement* discusses elites.

The document as a whole is very critical of elites in all aspects of American life.[34] The presence of economic elites, controlling vast financial resources, is described as a threat to democracy. Further, it was claimed that "[t]he influence of corporate elites on foreign policy is neither reliable nor democratic."[35] Labor elites also receive their share of criticism, being portrayed as complacent, co-opted, and largely out of touch with their rank-and-file members.[36] In the view of Hayden and his coauthors, business elites combine with military elites to form the military-industrial complex of which President Eisenhower had warned the nation as he left office.[37]

Thus, elites are seen as powerful, undemocratic, and responsible to no one. But the paradox is not far from the surface, and it was well captured by Viorst, who observed that the *Statement* "seemed to be saying, critical as it was of other elites, that a student elite had now to be forged on the campuses to realize the New Left's vision of the future."[38]

The agents for change were clearly intended to be college students, an elite group themselves, but not even the majority of students were seen as eligible for this role, preoccupied as they were in quests for beer, sex, grades, and social acceptance. Rather, social change would be brought about only by a minority among college students—an elite within an elite. As the document states in a major section headed "The Students," "Thousands of American students demonstrated that they at least felt the urgency of the times."[39] These thousands, seen against the backdrop of hundreds of thousands of American college students, are an elite group, indeed. Combined with the attack on elites discussed above, they produce the third paradox to be found in the *Statement*: elites are bad for the country, but the only possibilities for significant change lie in the hands of an elite group of activist college students.

The final paradox involves the role of the university in American life. Does higher education contribute to the problems discussed in *The Port Huron Statement*, or will the universities be instrumental in solving those problems? Not surprisingly, the SDS answer to both of those questions was affirmative.

The *Statement's* indictment of universities was thorough and scathing. Tom Hayden acknowledged, several years after Port Huron, that "the university was a more powerful issue in forming SDS than any other . . . the thing that was the most important source of alienation in the environment of my generation, what we were concerned with, was the campus."[40]

Hayden and the others directed their attack on several aspects of university life. Faculty members were portrayed as fearful of controversy and uncommitted.[41] Academic writing, on those occasions when it did focus on matters of real political concern, was seen as increasingly tentative—for which read "cowardly"—in its conclusions.[42] Universities were accused of inculcating apathy in their students and of setting up student governments based on "political pretense."[43] Universities prepare students for citizenship, Hayden and his colleagues wrote, "through perpetual rehearsals and, usually, through emasculation of what creative spirit there is in the individual."[44]

Despite these criticisms, however, *The Port Huron Statement* also portrayed the universities as the most likely base for social change in the country. Four advantages of these institutions were discussed. Universities, it was argued, occupy "a permanent position of social influence" in America."[45] Also, in this culture, universities are primary sources of information; they produce it, analyze it, and disseminate it. Further, for this reason, the power structure relies on universities, which are thus in a position to affect it profoundly. Finally, universities are open to people of all political persuasions, including the Left.[46] This analysis of the higher education system in the *Statement* completes the final paradox: the document both indicts the universities and depicts them as the main hope for fundamental social change.

Thus, while *The Port Huron Statement* accused American culture of being grounded in paradox, its authors seem to have based their own arguments on a series of intrinsically paradoxical ideas. It may be that this was inevitable, given the rhetorical stance taken by the students. The rhetoric of modern social movements lends itself to paradoxical worldview, as Karlyn Kohrs Campbell demonstrated in her studies of modern feminism. She contended that "feminist advocacy wavers between the rhetorical and the non-rhetorical, the persuasive and the non-persuasive."[47] This represents a paradoxical stance taken by feminists, but Campbell also demonstrates that such a stance leads to paradoxical rhetoric, as well: "The rhetoric of women's liberation appeals to *what are said to be* shared moral values, but forces recognition that these values are *not* shared."[48] She has argued elsewhere that modern feminism is characterized by two contradictory ideas (womanhood and personhood) held in dynamic tension.[49]

It seems reasonable that the viewpoint of the social reformer (as opposed to the revolutionary, who has the luxury of absolutes) will give rise to a rhetoric of paradox. Chesebro has argued that "periods of cultural unrest may be more thoughtfully explained by way of a paradoxical perspective."[50] If so, this may grant a degree of heuristic value to the foregoing analysis of *The Port Huron Statement*. Hayden and his coauthors saw much that was wrong with America, but they also saw great potential for peaceful social change. As the decade of the 1960s approached its end, the rhetoric of SDS would change greatly, as the next chapter discusses.

NOTES

1. Anthony Obershall, "The Decline of the 1960s Social Movements," in *Research in Social Movements, Conflicts and Change*, ed. Louis Friesberg (Greenwich, CT: JAI Press, 1978), 263.

2. Frederick D. Miller, "The End of SDS and the Emergence of Weatherman: Demise through Success," in *Social Movements of the Sixties and Seventies*, ed. Jo Freeman (New York: Longman Press, 1983), 284.

3. James Gilbert, "The Left Young and Old," *Partisan Review* 36 (1969): 352.

4. Edward P. Morgan, *The 60s Experience* (Philadelphia, PA: Temple University Press, 1991), 94.

5. Stewart Burns, *Social Movements of the 1960s* (Boston: Twayne, 1990), 57.

6. Kirkpatrick Sale, *SDS* (New York: Random House, 1973), 53–54.

7. Sale, 69.

8. Theodore Otto Windt, Jr., *Presidents and Protesters* (Tuscaloosa, AL: University of Alabama Press, 1990), 174.

9. Howard S. Erlich, "Populist Rhetoric Reassessed: A Paradox," *Quarterly Journal of Speech* 63 (1977): 150.

10. James W. Chesebro, "The Symbolic Construction of Social Realities: A Case Study in the Rhetorical Criticism of Paradox," *Communication Quarterly* 32 (1984): 165.

11. "The Port Huron Statement," reprinted in James Miller, *"Democracy is in the Streets": From Port Huron to the Siege of Chicago* (New York: Simon & Schuster, 1987), 330. Referred to hereafter as *Statement*.

12. Ibid.

13. Milton Viorst, *Fire in the Streets* (New York: Simon and Schuster, 1979), 195.

14. *Statement*, 332.

15. Ibid.

16. Todd Gitlin, *The Sixties: Years of Hope, Days of Rage* (New York: Bantam Books, 1987), 108.

17. *Statement*, 332.

18. Ibid.

19. Ibid., 333.

20. Ibid.

21. Ibid., 345.

22. Ibid., 359.

23. Alan Adelson, *SDS* (New York: Charles Scribner's Sons, 1972), 206.

24. Viorst, 194.

25. Gitlin, 121.

26. *Statement*, 350.

27. Ibid., 337.

28. Ibid.

29. Ibid., 350.

30. Ibid.

31. Ibid.

32. Ibid., 351.

33. Ibid.

34. Nancy Zaroulis and Gerald Sullivan, *Who Spoke Up?* (Garden City, NY: Doubleday, 1984), 30.

35. *Statement*, 363.

36. Ibid., 344.

37. Ibid., 340.

38. Viorst, 193.

39. *Statement*, 333.

40. Quoted in Viorst, 193.

41. Ibid., 346.

42. Ibid.

43. Ibid., 334.

44. Ibid.

45. Ibid., 373.

46. Ibid.

47. Karlyn Kohrs Campbell, "The Rhetoric of Women's Liberation: An Oxymoron," *Quarterly Journal of Speech* 59 (1973): 84.

48. Ibid., 85.

49. Karlyn Kohrs Campbell, "Femininity and Feminism: To Be or Not to Be a Woman," *Communication Quarterly* 31 (1983): 103.

50. Chesebro, 170.

Chapter Seven

Bringing the War Home: The Rhetoric of the Weathermen

As noted in the preceding chapter, the founding of SDS and its early development were based on general agreement concerning basic values, such as social justice, racial equality, and participatory democracy. Seven years after the adoption of *The Port Huron Statement*, however, SDS would fall apart in an atmosphere of acrimonious ideological conflict. That bitter dispute gave birth to an entity that has been called "the most extravagant development of the politics of the Sixties"[1] as well as "a force unlike any ever seen before in America"[2]: the Weathermen. This chapter analyzes the rhetoric of the Weathermen[3] as manifested in the three phases of the group's development, discusses some noteworthy features of Weathermen rhetoric, and examines several effects of the use of that rhetoric. But first, some background is in order.

SDS membership grew throughout the 1960s, especially after the organization's main concern shifted from civil rights to the Vietnam War in 1965. As the number and diversity of active members increased, disagreements over political ideology began to appear; *The Port Huron Statement* ceased to be everyone's guiding light. One of the strongest voices within SDS came to be that of the Progressive Labor (PL) coalition. As the Progressive Labor Party, it had existed for years on its own—a tightly organized, well-disciplined organization dedicated to achieving peaceful socialist revolution by mobilizing the nation's industrial workers.[4]

Beginning in 1966, PL members began to join SDS in large numbers, and by 1969 it was threatening to become the dominant voice within the organization; along with its size, PL was expert at political infighting, and its members usually got their way at SDS chapter meetings and national conventions. Many other members of SDS viewed this with alarm and anger, for several reasons. One was that PL, as noted, was worker oriented, not student oriented. The concerns of college students, who were still the majority within SDS, were of little interest to the older, more traditional PL members.[5]

Another aspect of PL that disturbed many in SDS was its political orientation. For a Leftist group, it was relatively conservative. PL did not support the North Vietnamese in their war against the United States, it did not seek ties with Castro's Cuba, as some SDS members did, and it had little use for the Black Panthers, a revolutionary group based in northern ghettos with which SDS had informal ties.[6]

Consequently, opposition to PL began to develop among some other SDS members. The largest of the dissenting factions was the Radical Youth Movement (RYM). Actually, RYM was itself split due to disagreements over abstruse points of political dogma into two loosely allied groups: RYM I and RYM II.[7]

A crisis occurred at the SDS national convention in June 1969. The various factions within the organization came prepared to debate and harangue each other, but RYM I was ready to go beyond mere disputation. The RYM I delegates distributed a long position paper with a title taken from a Bob Dylan song: "You Don't Need a Weatherman to Know Which Way the Wind Blows." The document, discussed below, polarized the convention even further, if that were possible. Then the RYM I leaders secured the support of the SDS–allied Black Panthers, whose Illinois "minister of information" berated PL from the podium, reading a statement that had been authorized by Panther leader Eldridge Cleaver. The minister of information concluded by saying, "If the Progressive Labor Party continues its egocentric policies and revisionist behavior, they will be considered as counter-revolutionary traitors and will be dealt with as such."[8]

Then Bernadine Dohrn came to the microphone. One of three SDS national secretaries, she was also one of the authors of the RYM I "Weatherman" paper. She, too, denounced PL, "quoting, citing, pinning, slashing, a performance so masterful that at least one person was convinced it must have been prepared days in advance."[9] Then she took the next, bold, step, proclaiming, "SDS can no longer live with people who are objectively racist, anticommunist, and reactionary. Progressive Labor Party members, people in the Worker-Student Alliance, and all others who do not accept our principles . . . are no longer members of SDS." Her last line, shouted before storming off the stage, was a slogan from Chinese Communist leader Lin Piao, and an omen of things to come: "Long live the victory of people's war!"[10]

With this purge, SDS effectively destroyed itself. PL and its sympathizers were expelled, and many others, adherents of neither PL nor RYM I, quit the organization in disgust. All that remained were the diehards of RYM I, who soon took a new name—a reflection of the title given to their founding statement—and became the Weathermen.

PHASE 1: IN THE STREETS

This initial period of activity by the Weathermen was characterized by several types of open, revolutionary activity. But it seems appropriate first to examine the Weathermen's initial rhetorical effort, the document entitled "You Don't Need a Weatherman to Know Which Way the Wind Blows." This position paper, written by eleven people (five of whom, Bernadine Dohrn, Bill Ayers, John Jacobs, Terry Robbins, and Mark Rudd, would become national leaders of the organization), both predicts and explains much of the activity that would soon follow in what I have called Phase 1. As Edward Bacciocco, Jr., wrote, "The eagerness to use violent rhetoric reflected a willingness to engage in physical violence."[11]

The Weathermen position paper begins by defining the sides in conflict: "The main struggle going on in the world today is between US [sic] imperialism and the national liberation struggles against it."[12] The group's "founding parents" had no doubts in their minds about where the contest should lead: "The goal is the destruction of US [sic] imperialism and the achievement of a classless world: world communism."[13] This effort was being carried out, the document argued, internationally by Third World revolutionary movements, especially the North Vietnamese. At home, the main force opposing American imperialism would be black America, which the document refers to as the "Black Colony" in America.[14] The role of white revolutionaries such as the Weathermen was to support and assist the coming black revolution.

The oppressive arm of domestic American imperialism is referred to as "the pigs" (a slang term of the period for police, although the Weathermen would soon broaden its scope to include anyone who failed to support their positions). The position paper said, "Our job is not to avoid the issue of the pigs as 'diverting' from anti-imperialist struggle, but to emphasize that they are our real enemy if we fight that struggle to win."[15]

These themes, and others, are developed in the document's forty pages—hardly a model of either conciseness, elegance, or logic. As Carl Oglesby, an SDS veteran who had opposed the Weathermen, observed:

Any close reading of the RYM's Weatherman statement will drive you blind. Sometimes the vanguard [of the upcoming revolution] is the black ghetto community, sometimes only the Panthers, sometimes the Third World as a whole, sometimes only the Vietnamese, and sometimes only the Lao Dong party. Sometimes [the concept of a revolutionary vanguard] is a seriously Hegelian concept, referring vaguely to all earthly manifestations of the spirit of revolution. At still

other times, it seems to be the fateful organ of that radicalized industrial pro-
letariat (USA) which has yet to make its Cold War–era debut.[16]

As rhetoric, the first Weathermen statement was not likely to win
many friends or influence a large number of people. The document,
both in language and substance, "creates a sense of distance, exclusion,
and elitism," the polar opposite of *The Port Huron Statement* of seven
years earlier.[17] Further, the position paper was not even intended to
attract a broad spectrum of SDS members since it held the proper role
of white, middle-class revolutionaries to be that of squire to the knight
of Third World and black American revolution—and this knight was
likely to have singularly little use for white, middle-class college students
once the struggle had been won.[18]

The document did serve some rhetorical purposes for those inclined
toward the Weathermen line, however. The jargon-laden, abstruse political theory of the statement "served to distract from intractable realities—above all, the widespread public distaste for revolutionary
violence. Murk enabled the sectarians to mask (even for themselves)
what they intended to do."[19]

In addition, the position paper served as an in-group reference point
for those who would become committed to the cause of the Weathermen.
For others within SDS and elsewhere, the statement was as impenetrable
as the Dead Sea Scrolls; for the followers of Bernadine Dohrn and her
cohorts, it quickly became Holy Writ. As Todd Gitlin argued,

The prefabricated phrases [of the Weathermen statement] spare the trouble of
genuine thought, but more: they are easily parroted by those who want to feel
privy to Important Questions. They are like a tourist's handbook phrases, in-
stantly conveying a false sense of membership in an alien culture—in this case,
the culture of World Revolution.[20]

The Weathermen, in short, devised "a rhetoric and practice of fe-
rocity."[21] The rhetoric had its beginnings at the final SDS convention;
the practice was soon to follow.

In what I have called Phase 1, the Weathermen engaged in several
different kinds of public activity designed to advance their revolutionary
agenda. These activities were all in some sense rhetorical since they
were intended to attract people to the fledgling movement. As the original Weathermen statement admitted, "No revolutionary party could
possibly survive without relying on the active support and participation
of masses of people."[22]

The "mass of people" from whom the Weathermen hoped to recruit
consisted of disadvantaged urban white youth. Most college students,
the reasoning went, were by definition too bourgeois to be made into

dedicated revolutionaries; they already had too great a stake in the power structure. But those who had never been to college, and who were unlikely ever to go, were seen as much better material. As Weathermen leader Bill Ayers put it, working-class teenagers "hate their jobs, hate their schools, hate their parents, hate the authorities. . . . These kids who dropped out of high school are more perceptive than those of us who went through college."[23]

The Weathermen's Phase 1 activities were directed at this audience. Although not rhetoric in the narrowly traditional sense, all of these actions were devised to interest, attract, and recruit disaffected lower-class teens. To this end were designed confrontations, "jailbreaks," and, finally, the "Days of Rage."

Although at first a seemingly curious tactic, the confrontation involved pitting Weathermen against the very people who were their target audience. In short, a group of Weathermen would go to a working-class neighborhood and invade a location where the young were known to hang out: a park, a beach, or a fast-food restaurant, for example. The revolutionaries would then harangue the locals, and, when the latter responded with hostility, fight them. The idea was that the children of the poor were likely to be impressed by only one thing the Weathermen had to offer: toughness.[24] After the fisticuffs, "[t]he youths would then presumably respect the revolutionaries, become curious . . . and be open to being organized into a citywide revolutionary youth movement."[25]

During the summer of 1969, Weathermen groups were active in a number of northern cities, such as Columbus, Detroit, and Pittsburgh, all employing basically the same confrontational tactics, along with "jailbreaks," to attract white, underclass youth. In Cambridge, Massachusetts, a variation was employed when a group of twenty Weathermen invaded Harvard University's Center for International Affairs, which was reputed to be involved in war-related research. They vandalized the facility and physically attacked everyone in sight, including several faculty members. Thereafter, Weathermen around the country used this incident as a point of pride in their recruitment efforts, on the assumption that poor white kids were full of class hatred for the Ivy League.[26]

The spirit of the Harvard raid was also embodied in what the Weathermen called "jailbreaks." These were designed to reach white working-class young people in the places where they spent the most time while enjoying it the least: the schools. Although most of these assaults involved high schools, the first took place at McComb Community College outside Detroit. The Weathermen, perhaps revealing unconscious class snobbery of their own, assumed that community college students were sufficiently "working class" to be grist for the revolutionary mill.[27] A group of nine women entered a classroom at the college, interrupting a final examination. They took turns delivering their revolutionary message and assaulted two people who tried to leave. A faculty member called the police, and the women were arrested.[28]

Other jailbreaks were conducted at high schools around the country that spring and fall. The typical approach to these actions had a group of Weathermen or, more precisely, Weatherwomen, since for some reason the participants tended to be female, entering a high school in a working-class area where they would run through the halls shouting "Jailbreak!" The assumption embodied in the slogan was that the students saw their schools as prisons and would thus welcome the "liberation" offered by the Weatherwomen. Leaflets would be distributed, and sometimes classrooms would be invaded à la McComb. In some instances, the Weatherwomen would lift their tops and display their breasts, to show their contempt for bourgeois social mores. Inevitably, the police would be summoned. Sometimes the invaders would manage to leave before the authorities could arrive. On other occasions, the police would take the radicals into custody, but not without a fight. The Weathermen always fought, adhering to their doctrine that the students would be impressed by toughness.[29]

Were these youngsters inspired by the Weathermen's combination of Marxist rhetoric and street brawling? The answer is that generally they were not. Neither the confrontations nor the jailbreaks brought many teenagers into the Weathermen's fold. Indeed, the reaction to all this revolutionary activity was generally quite negative. As Irwin Unger and Debi Unger observed, "The forays only convinced most street kids that the radical students were crazy."[30] The confrontations usually resulted in the Weathermen instigators being beaten up by the teenagers, without obtaining their respect. The jailbreaks were also counterproductive; not only did the high school students not rush to join the revolution, they often supported their teachers' efforts to get the Weathermen arrested. In one jailbreak site, Boston's English High School, the students did stage a rally the next day—but to protest the Weathermen, not the establishment. As prominent Leftist Dave Dellinger remarked, "It was no mean accomplishment in those days to unite high school kids and their administrators against critics of the schools and the war"—but the Weathermen had done it.[31]

In their rhetoric to each other (such as the holdover SDS publication *New Left Notes*), the Weathermen grasped at whatever rhetorical straws they could to describe the confrontations and jailbreaks as successful. For example, the disastrous effort at McComb Community College was described in *New Left Notes* as an illustration of what glories can be accomplished "when women exercise real power."[32] Despite all the self-congratulatory rhetoric, however, there was a sense among many

Weathermen that the current level of struggle was insufficient. This led to the planning for what would become known as the Days of Rage.

The Days of Rage, also known to the Weathermen as the National Action, referred to four days of demonstrations and other activities to take place in Chicago from October 8–11, 1969. Chicago was chosen for two symbolic reasons. First, it had been the site of the "police riot" (the Walker Commission's term) against demonstrators during the 1968 Democratic National Convention. The Weathermen's view was that the Left had lost that round and that it was time for round 2. A second reason for the selection of Chicago was that the trial of the "Chicago Eight" (later the "Chicago Seven") was scheduled to begin there in late September. The leaders of the major organizations involved in the 1968 convention protests, such as SDS, the Yippies, and the Black Panthers, had been indicted on federal conspiracy charges and were to be tried as a group. The Weathermen wanted the Days of Rage to be a commentary on that trial. They also expected the national media to be in town to cover the trial and thus to give wide publicity to dramatic protests against it.

The Weathermen hyped the proposed National Action to each other and to potential supporters for the two months preceding. Big things were expected. An article in *New Left Notes* proclaimed: "On October 11, tens of thousands of people will come to Chicago to bring the war home. Join us."[33]

The grandiose predictions were not realized. The total attendance of active protesters was between 600 and 800.[34] A blow-by-blow account of the Weathermen's activities during those four days in October is unnecessary here and readily available elsewhere.[35] A brief description will suffice before we consider the more important issue of its rhetorical impact.

On October 7, the day before the protest was due to begin, some Weathermen blew up a statue of a policeman in Chicago's Haymarket Square. The Chicago police, who held no love for demonstrators at the best of times, were greatly angered by this desecration of a memorial to the officers who had died while quelling the Haymarket Riot of 1886.[36]

The next evening, a group of about 300 Weathermen rampaged through Chicago's Gold Coast, an affluent business and residential area, breaking windows and trashing cars. When the police moved in, the protesters, many wearing helmets and protective clothing and carrying clubs, fought back. When it was over, seventy-five Weathermen were under arrest and twenty-one police officers were injured.[37]

The next morning, a group of between 50 and 100 female Weathermen led by Bernadine Dohrn formed in Grant Park and marched off with the expressed intention of attacking a nearby Selective Service Induction

Center. When police ordered them to halt, some of the women charged. Twelve were subdued and taken into custody; police injuries were minor.

Several actions planned for the next day were called off while the remaining Weathermen (absent the arrested, the injured, and those who had given up and left town) licked their wounds and reassessed. The fact that the governor of Illinois had sent National Guard troops into Chicago may have influenced this mood of caution.[38]

On Saturday, October 11, the final demonstration took place. Just after noon, a group of about twenty Weathermen entered Haymarket Square. They were confronted by police, fought, and were arrested. Shortly thereafter, a large group of about 300 protesters moved into the square. They listened to speeches for half an hour, then moved off *en masse*, followed by a large contingent of police. At a prearranged verbal signal, the marchers suddenly dashed down Madison Avenue, breaking windows and fighting with the police who tried to arrest them.[39] Property damage was relatively minor, and 180 Weathermen were arrested.[40]

As usual, the Weathermen after-action rhetoric was designed to put the best face on things. At the end of the Days of Rage, a Weatherman orator told his remaining comrades, "We have shown the pigs that we can fight. We have shown the pigs that they have overextended themselves on another front. We have taken the movement a qualitative step forward."[41] In a lengthy article published in *Leviathan*, the Weathermen's successor to *New Left Notes*, written after Chicago, Weatherman Shin'ya Ono provided a detailed account of the preparations for the action and the action itself. Then he judged the Days of Rage "in as objective a way as possible."[42] Not surprisingly, Ono saw the action as a success in every way. Much damage had been inflicted on the city and its police force, Ono said. Many young people were supposedly contemplating joining the revolution as a result of the Weathermen's example. The wimps in the rest of the antiwar movement, said Ono, had been inspired to go back to their own schools and "kick ass," and the action had transformed the Weathermen themselves into full-fledged revolutionaries.[43]

By any standard more objective than Ono's, however, the Days of Rage deserved to be called the Days of Mild Annoyance. This appears especially true when one considers the rhetorical objective of the National Action. The target audience for the Weathermen's revolutionary message remained impoverished white youth, and one of the main goals of Chicago was to get these "street kids" *into* the streets. As Stuart Daniels noted, "The Weathermen were hoping to inspire others to join in the struggle against American imperialism—the actions of Days of Rage can be seen as exemplary in intention."[44] If so, it was an example not followed. The Weathermen had confidently predicted that more than

10,000 young revolutionaries would descend on Chicago like avenging angels; the actual number, at its highest estimate, was 800. Further, there were no new recruits to be had from the city's white poor. "White slum kids, if they noticed the Weatherman tactics in Chicago at all, would have considered them amateurish and stupid."[45]

In addition to the failure to gain new recruits, the Weathermen faced a retention problem, as well. A number of people who had come to Chicago as committed Weathermen left at various points during the Days of Rage, never to return to the fold. Some had decided the Weathermen's political style was too reminiscent of fascism; others saw some of the actions as pointless.[46]

Contrary to Shin'ya Ono's argument that the Days of Rage had put steel in the spines and clubs in the hands of the rest of the antiwar movement, the truth is that Chicago cost the Weathermen what little support they had among the Left.[47] As Nicholas Strinkowski's analysis of the Weathermen's organizational functioning showed, "The most serious cost of the Days of Rage was alienation from the rest of the political Left. . . . This violent and seemingly pointless street action would cost the group much of the external support, both physical and ideological, that was necessary to maintain a large organization."[48] Even the Black Panthers, whom the Weathermen admired so much, viewed the action with scorn. Panther leader Fred Hampton publicly denounced the Days of Rage as "stupid," "adventuristic," and "Custeristic."[49]

If the Weathermen achieved any of their rhetorical goals in Chicago, it was notoriety. As was anticipated, the national news media were in town for the Chicago Eight trial, and the Weathermen's activities provided great copy. The reporters, many of whom had been unfamiliar with the Weathermen before Chicago, tended to take the group's rhetoric at face value and wrote stories greatly exaggerating the revolutionaries' importance.[50] The press created a myth of the Weathermen as a large, nationwide, well-equipped group of revolutionaries who posed a serious threat to the country.[51] The Weathermen were gratified by this coverage, but it served them no useful purpose. The myth did not make Americans more willing to support or surrender in the face of the Weathermen's idea of revolution. It did create widespread concern, and this proved a fertile climate for government repression.

Two months after Chicago, the Weathermen held a "war council" in Flint, Michigan. About 400 people attended to hear the group's ruling council, the "Weather Bureau," announce a change in policy for the organization. Public rhetoric notwithstanding, the "blatant failure" of the Days of Rage to attract new converts to the cause of revolution had affected Weathermen leaders greatly and led to a change in philosophy.[52] Instead of trying to win over the populace, the Weathermen would separate themselves from the people by going underground to continue the struggle. Instead of trying to grow larger, the organization would pare itself down, purging two-thirds of its members, thus becoming small enough to function in secret. Instead of public brawling, the new tactic would emphasize clandestine bombing.[53]

The oratory announcing these decisions was consistent with the new policy itself—it stressed separation rather than unity, and hatred for practically everyone, instead of love for anyone. At the Flint meeting, "the Weathermen displayed a rhetorical tone that reached a new peak of irrational violence."[54] Bernadine Dohrn extolled to the assembled would-be revolutionaries the actions of a certain young man who had been much in the news: Charles Manson. "Dig it; first they killed those pigs, then they ate dinner in the room with them, then they even shoved a fork into pig Tate's stomach. Wild!"[55] Mark Rudd described his battles with police in Chicago, saying "It's a wonderful feeling to hit a pig." He then speculated, "It must be a really wonderful feeling to kill a pig or blow up a building."[56] Another Weathermen leader, John Jacobs, tried to express his philosophy of the revolution: "We're against everything that's 'good and decent' in honky America. We will burn and loot and destroy."[57] Later, a debate actually arose over whether it would be politically valid to kill white babies before they could grow up to become oppressor pig imperialists. Some of the assemblage were aghast at this notion, but at least one Weatherman responded by shouting, "All white babies are pigs."[58] All told, the "war council" was no less than "a ritual of political diabolism."[59] It seemed an oddly fitting transition into the next phase of the Weathermen's efforts at revolution.

PHASE 2: UNDER THE GROUND

This next phase of Weathermen activity, which lasted eleven months, was characterized by what Ronald Fraser called "armed propaganda."[60] During this period, the Weathermen communicated with the world at large principally through the use of high explosives.

Apart from whatever damage might be done, the bombs served a rhetorical purpose. They were always set off at a location somehow connected with what the Weathermen considered "pig Amerika [sic]." Further, the bombs were usually planted in response to some new development, either in the war or in what the Weathermen perceived as imperialist repression at home. An "affinity group"[61] in New York City set off fire bombs at the home of Judge John M. Murtagh, who was presiding at a major trial of Black Panthers. An explosive device went off inside New York City police headquarters; another exploded in Albany, at the offices of the New York State Department of Corrections, in retaliation for the brutal suppression of the Attica prison riot. After the White House ordered an increase in the bombing of North Vietnam, the Weathermen planted a bomb of their own in a Pentagon lavatory. Another bomb went off in a washroom at the Capitol when Congress refused to pass legislation to eliminate all appropriations for the war effort. Other bombings commented on similar political points.[62]

In much of this activity, the element of retaliation was strong. Bill Ayers, a member of the Weather Bureau, later explained the campaign:

We felt that being able to do things like the bombing of the Capitol and the bombing of the Pentagon would wear them down. They were related to when the United States government bombed Laos and when they invaded Cambodia. We felt that they would have to pay a price for those kinds of crimes. Our point was that we live in the mother country of imperialism and that we have access to places and technology, so if you make the world unsafe for everybody else, we'll make the world unsafe for you.[63]

Dave Dellinger wrote of the Weathermen's bombing campaign that "[t]hey chose their targets with exquisite symbolism and exemplary care to avoid human injury."[64] If a bomb planted in an occupied building was set to go off during working hours, someone from the affinity group would call in a bomb threat so that people could be evacuated. In a way, this is curious, since the people in such buildings were almost certain to fit the Weathermen's definition of "pigs," and "off [kill] the pigs" had been one of the group's favorite slogans for some time. Perhaps even the Weathermen found cold-blooded murder easier to deal with theoretically and rhetorically than in practice.

Some deaths were associated with Weathermen bombings, however. In the summer of 1970, a truck bomb exploded outside the Mathematics Research Center at the University of Wisconsin, damaging the building where some war-related research was conducted and killing a graduate student who was working late. The media called this another Weatherman action, as did some historians of the period.[65] In fact, however, the bomb was placed by a group called the "New Year's Gang," which was not part of the Weathermen, although its members were sympathetic with the latter's goals.[66]

The only fatalities coming from Weathermen bombs were Weathermen themselves. On March 6, 1970, an elegant town house in New York City's Greenwich Village blew up, killing three people. The building belonged to businessman James Wilkerson, who was away on vacation—apparently unaware that his daughter Cathy was a dedicated Weatherman. Indeed, the Wilkerson home was the temporary refuge for the affinity group that had set off incendiary devices at the residence of Judge Murtagh.

The bodies were those of Diana Oughton, Ted Gold, and Terry Robbins. Cathy Wilkerson escaped from the rubble. Police and federal investigators combed the remains of the townhouse, and what they found led them to conclude that the Weathermen's avoidance of deliberate homicide was due for a change. The bombs under construction apparently included small charges of dynamite covered by roofing nails. They were, in short, "antipersonnel bombs."[67] Future Weathermen bombings (and they continued for several months more) conformed to the old strategy, however: the targets were buildings, not people.

The townhouse explosion and loss of three comrades unnerved the Weather Bureau leadership, and its members spent some months reconsidering the state of the revolution.[68] Out of this assessment came a new concept of the Weathermen's target audience. From disadvantaged white urban youths, the focus shifted to the members of what was loosely referred to as the "counterculture." In Weathermen communiques of this period, one can see references to drug use as a revolutionary practice, along with praise of "freaks," as members of the counterculture sometimes called themselves. A Weathermen message that appeared in July 1970 reflected the beginning of this shift:

We fight in many ways. Dope is one of our weapons. The laws against marijuana mean that millions of us are outlaws long before we actually split. Guns and grass are united in the youth underground.

Freaks are revolutionaries and revolutionaries are freaks. If you want to find us, this is where we are. In every tribe, commune, dormitory, farmhouse, barracks and townhouse where kids are making love, smoking dope and loading guns—fugitives from Amerikan [sic] justice are free to go.[69]

The significance of this enthusiasm for marijuana is clearer when it is contrasted with the previous Weathermen policy of forbidding drug use in the various affinity groups.[70] Apart from occasional group LSD trips (to build comradeship within the unit), the Weathermen were supposed to stay clean for the revolution.

One of the reasons for the Weathermen's interest in the counterculture is that many of its members were already (loosely) organized into communes, farms, "families," or "tribes." The Weathermen hoped to turn this existing organizational structure, such as it was, to a revolutionary purpose.[71]

To build a constituency among the "hippies," the Weathermen staged a "jailbreak" of a more literal kind. In September 1970, they helped Timothy Leary escape from a minimum-security prison in California, where he was serving time on drug charges. Leary, a former Harvard professor, had gained fame as an outspoken advocate of drug use, especially LSD. His rescuers provided him a false passport and helped him escape to Algeria, from which he could not be extradited.

In the communique justifying this action, Bernadine Dohrn described

Leary as "a political prisoner, captured for the work he did in helping all of us begin the task of creating a new culture." She went on to claim that "LSD and grass . . . will help us make a future world where it will be possible to live in peace."[72] As Peter Collier and David Horowitz pointed out, "The Weather Underground's participation in the escape showed the new direction its leadership had determined to follow."[73] That new direction led the Weathermen into the final stage of their existence.

PHASE 3: ON THE WANE

The beginning of this last act of the Weathermen drama is easy to date with some precision; the end is harder to pinpoint. In December 1970, Bernadine Dohrn, on behalf of the Weather Bureau, issued a position paper explaining the new Weathermen philosophy. The document was entitled "New Morning—Changing Weather," after another Bob Dylan song, and appeared to indicate that the Weathermen had, of all things, begun to mellow.[74]

Dohrn admitted that, in their reliance on dynamite as the means of bringing on the revolution, the Weathermen had fallen into a "military error."[75] She continued:

The townhouse accident forever destroyed our belief that armed struggle is the only really revolutionary struggle. It is time for the movement to go out into the air, to organize, to risk calling rallies and demonstrations, to convince that mass actions against the war and in support of rebellions do make a difference. . . . A group of outlaws who are isolated from the youth community do not have a sense of what is going on, cannot develop strategies that grow to include large numbers of people. . . . People become revolutionaries in the schools, in the army, in communes, and on the streets. Not in an underground cell.[76]

Thus, for the first time in their brief history, the Weathermen adopted something like a traditional rhetorical perspective. They had a somewhat more realistic conception of the intended audience (an amalgam of counterculture "freaks" and the kind of conventional Leftists whom they had read out of SDS in the first place).[77] Further, in this period the Weathermen engaged in their most mainstream rhetorical efforts. In 1974, they published on their own printing press a 186-page book called *Prairie Fire* (after the revolutionary slogan, "A single spark can start a prairie fire"), which contained essays, poems, and the Weathermen's interpretation of the history of the New Left in America.[78] This was followed in 1975–76 by six issues of a journal called *Osawatome* (from the Indian name of abolitionist John Brown), as well as bimonthly publication of *The Fire Next Time*, the latest incarnation of SDS's defunct *New Left Notes*. Counterculture newspapers such as *The Berkeley Tribe* also published writings by Weathermen.[79]

In 1975, the members of the Weather Bureau even became movie stars, of a sort. Oscar-winning director Emile DeAntonio, who knew someone in touch with Mark Rudd, made a documentary about the Weathermen's experience in exile. The film, entitled *Underground*, was released the following year. Mostly it consists of a series of low-key polemics from Bernadine Dohrn, Bill Ayers, Jeff Jones, and the others, intercut with clips that illustrate and support some of the more reasonable assertions (such as footage of police beating striking workers in the 1920s, and an interview with the widow of Black Panther leader Fred Hampton shortly after he was gunned down by police). The location of the film was not revealed and was referred to only as a "safe house," and the Weathermen participants carefully avoided showing their faces to the camera— they were filmed mostly through a muslin curtain that made their features unrecognizable.

This brief foray "above ground" may have encouraged the members of the Weather Bureau to go further. They attempted to re-involve themselves in mainstream protest, this time by proxy. The Prairie Fire Organizing Committee (PFOC) was formed by cohorts of the Weathermen who were not under indictment and thus able to move about freely. The members of the steering committee were handpicked by Bernadine Dohrn and included her sister, Jennifer. The PFOC planned a convention, the "Hard Times Conference," for January 1976 in Chicago. It was hoped that the conference would be well attended and would ratify the Weathermen's revised political agenda. The first expectation was realized; the second was not.[80]

Many of the two thousand people attending the conference did not agree with the Weathermen's new and improved mainstream politics. Dohrn's surrogates quickly lost control of the agenda, and the Weather Bureau members, who were listening to the proceedings over the radio, were aghast to hear resolutions being passed that condemned their recent actions, repudiated their political outlook, and accused them of "crimes against national liberation struggles, women and the anti-imperialist left."[81]

Over the ensuing weeks, all members of the Weather Bureau were purged from the new organization they had created. The PFOC limped along for another year without them, resuming the bombing campaign in the process, until its leaders were betrayed to the FBI by an undercover agent and arrested.[82] Dohrn, Rudd, Ayers, and the others gradually surfaced into society over the next few years. They were all arrested but served little jail time; the government's evidence against them was old, often weak, and in some cases tainted by illegal practices involved in obtaining it. Thus ended the Weathermen—not with the bang of dynamite, but with a whimper so faint it was heard by almost no one.

SOME OBSERVATIONS ON WEATHERMEN RHETORIC

Milton Cantor wrote of the Weathermen that "[t]he rhetoric of civil disobedience was . . . forgotten, drowned by the rhetoric of revolution—with isolation, political marginality, and intensified feelings of alienation resulting."[83] This is a reasonable assessment, but it tells little about the specifics of the Weathermen's "rhetoric of revolution." What follows are some characteristics of what Abe Peck calls the Weathermen's "verbal overkill."[84]

Demand for Instant Change

Revolutionaries are impatient people; they would not be revolutionaries otherwise. The Weathermen were no exception. Prior to its dissolution in 1969, SDS had been trying to get Washington to stop the war for five years. Conventional, law-abiding, peaceful protest had been employed, time and again, to no apparent effect. By the time the members of RYM I were ready to assume the mantle of the Weathermen, their impatience was such that instantaneous granting of all their demands would barely have been quick enough.[85] Since instant change is rarely, if ever, forthcoming from any political system, frustration for the Weathermen was inevitable, and frustration is the breeding ground for violence. As Laurence Lader wrote, "[The Left's] failure to stop the Vietnam War . . . created a mood of desperation, a crisis psychology that demanded instant results and instant revolution. The turn to violence and Weather's guerrilla army was one obvious result."[86]

Failure of Audience Adaptation

In light of what we have seen in this chapter about the Weathermen's rhetorical activities, even bringing up the idea of audience adaptation in this context may seem ludicrous. But we must remember that the Weathermen *wanted* to build some kind of mass movement; they just had no notion how to go about it. Much of their spoken and written rhetoric, for example, was full of quotations from contemporary Communist heroes: Mao, Lin Piao, Che Guevara, and General Giap, among others.[87] Assuming the average working-class American knew who most of these people were, he or she would likely be filled with revulsion at the thought of adopting Communist ideas. As mentioned in several chapters already and developed in Chapter 8, anti-Communism has long been a knee-jerk reaction for most Americans. The use of Communist sources to bolster one's rhetoric will thus be counterproductive unless the audience is already considerably left of the political center.

The protest actions of the Weathermen were also likely to be incomprehensible, at best, to the majority of Americans. As noted, the disadvantaged white youth who were for a time the Weathermen's prime audience were likely to regard fighting the police as stupid and pointless. The bombing campaign was also mystifying to most people: "The bombing of banks, corporate headquarters, courthouses, or Judge Murtagh's home had no direct relationship to the war, as far as most people were concerned."[88] All in all, the contemporaneous judgment made by Ralph Whitehead still seems justified: "The Weathermen, although they hope to lead the oppressed, don't care to talk directly to them first."[89]

Polarization

The Weathermen clearly lived in a Manichean universe. There was absolute Good (epitomized by the Weathermen and their cause) and utter Evil (everyone else). Such perceptions tend to make for easy, if simplistic, choices. The Weathermen had various dichotomies to offer in their rhetoric. One could either join with the oppressors, who were all white Americans—except for the Weathermen themselves—or the Liberators, people of color both at home and abroad.[90] This can be seen in the writing of Weatherman theoretician Shin'ya Ono. For the white workers, Ono said, "Their only choice is either joining the world revolution led by the blacks, the yellows and the browns, or being put down as US [sic] imperialist pigs by the people of the Third World."[91]

A favorite subject for the dichotomizing rhetoric of the Weathermen involved the other people in the antiwar movement. According to Shin'ya Ono, "Either we [on the Left] push on to become soldiers in the world revolutionary war, or we completely slide back to our respective bourgeois holes and become anti-Communist pigs."[92]

Of course, the act of naming can itself be polarizing. If you name something in a strongly negative way, then, by implication, its opposite must be strongly good. Thus, those on the Left who had chosen not to support the Weathermen's revolution had become, by virtue of their choice, "right wingers," "movement creeps," "wimpy," or "those old Movement people," thereby leaving the field of political virtue to the Weathermen alone.[93]

SOME EFFECTS OF WEATHERMEN RHETORIC

It seems needless abuse of a dead horse to say that the Weathermen's revolutionary rhetoric did not achieve any of their goals. Dave Dellinger points out the Weathermen's two fundamental errors:

First, they grossly overestimated the readiness of the American people, including large numbers of those opposed to the war, to accept revolutionary violence as a legitimate and necessary tactic in the American struggle. Second, they misread the number of anti-imperialists willing to follow the leadership of a dogmatic and authoritarian "vanguard."[94]

The Weathermen's inability to bring about a revolution does not mean, however, that their activities had no lasting effects. There were at least two.

One effect involved the rest of the antiwar movement, which the Weathermen all but destroyed. As noted, they took over one faction of SDS and, by splitting off, caused the rest of the organization to collapse. Moreover, Weathermen activities blackened the name of SDS in the public mind, since media reports frequently referred to the Weathermen as "the militant faction of SDS," or something similar.[95] But SDS was not locked in the pillory alone. All other antiwar organizations tended to be lumped together with the window-breaking, bomb-setting Weathermen in the public's perception. As Nancy Zaroulis and Gerald Sullivan argued, "The actions of a few score insanely angry youths besmirched the historical truth of years of peaceful effort by concerned, responsible, and patriotic citizens, youths and adults alike."[96]

Among those inclined to perceive all antiwar groups as occupying the same far-left end of the political spectrum as the Weathermen were many members of the Nixon administration.[97] This was the second effect of the Weathermen's violent rhetoric: it brought about a period of political repression that often left civil liberties in the dust. Much of this was clandestine: illegal wiretaps, harassing surveillance, and break-ins. Later these and similar tactics would be shifted from America's sworn enemies to Nixon's political foes, culminating in the Watergate scandal.[98]

But even the repressive measures that were more open met with no significant public outcry. The Weathermen were seen by much of the populace as such a major threat that whatever Nixon proposed to meet that threat would be accepted.[99] Thus, even though "civil liberties in the Nixon era were threatened at least as severely as during the McCarthy period of the 1950s,"[100] few Americans seemed very concerned—thanks to the Weathermen.

As we have seen, the Weathermen's activities were important, but not influential. They brought heat, but not light, to the controversy over the war; they had rage but no viable solutions. SDS founder Al Haber once wrote that "the power of the left is largely its ability to persuade."[101] But the Weathermen rejected this advice at the same time they abandoned SDS. For the Weathermen, rhetoric was seen less as a beacon than as a cudgel.

NOTES

1. Peter Collier and David Horowitz, *Destructive Generation* (New York: Summit Books, 1989), 69.

2. Kirkpatrick Sale, *SLS* (New York: Random House, 1973), 579.

3. This organization has been known by various names in its brief history: the Weathermen, Weatherman, the Weatherpeople (in response to charges of sexist language by several female Weather Persons), and, later, the Weather Underground. For the sake of simplicity, the term "the Weathermen" will be used throughout this chapter.

4. Frederick D. Miller, "The End of SDS and the Emergence of Weatherman: Demise through Success," in *Social Movements of the Sixties and Seventies*, ed. Jo Freeman (New York: Longman, 1983), 287.

5. Miller, 287.

6. Stuart Daniels, "The Weathermen," *Government and Opposition* 9 (1974): 434.

7. Todd Gitlin, *The Sixties: Years of Hope, Days of Rage* (New York: Bantam Books, 1987), 383.

8. Quoted in Lawrence Lader, *Power on the Left* (New York: W. W. Norton, 1979), 279.

9. Quoted in Sale, 574.

10. Ibid.

11. Edward J. Bacciocco, Jr., *The New Left in America* (Stanford, CA: Hoover Institution Press, 1974), 205.

12. Karin Ashley, Bill Ayers, Bernadine Dohrn, John Jacobs, Jeff Jones, Gerry Long, Howie Machtinger, Jim Mellen, Terry Robbins, Mark Rudd, and Steve Tappis, "You Don't Need a Weatherman to Know Which Way the Wind Blows," in *Weatherman*, ed. Harold Jacobs (New York: Ramparts Press, 1970), 51.

13. Ashley, et al., 53.

14. Ibid., 53–54.

15. Ibid., 84.

16. Carl Oglesby, "Notes on a Decade Ready for the Dustbin," in *Toward a History of the New Left*, ed. R. David Myers (New York: Carlson Publishing, 1989), 42.

17. Sale, 562–563.

18. Ibid., 563.

19. Gitlin, 390.

20. Ibid.

21. Todd Gitlin, *The Whole World is Watching* (Berkeley, CA: University of California Press, 1980), 191.

22. Ashley, et al., 89.

23. Quoted in John Kifner, "Vandals in the Mother Country," *The New York Times Magazine*, January 4, 1970, 16.

24. Irwin Unger, *The Movement* (New York: Dodd, Mead & Company, 1975), 167.

25. Kifner, 16.

26. Gitlin, *The Sixties*, 391.

27. Sale, 588.

28. Unger, 170.

29. Alan Adelson, *SDS* (New York: Charles Scribner's Sons, 1972), 246.

30. Irwin Unger and Debi Unger, *Turning Point: 1968* (New York: Charles Scribner's Sons, 1988), 294.

31. Dave Dellinger, *More Power Than We Know* (Garden City, NY: Anchor Press, 1975), 164.

32. "The Motor City Nine," in Jacobs, 161.

33. "Look at It: America, 1969," in Jacobs, 174.

34. Joan Morrison and Robert K. Morrison, *From Camelot to Kent State* (New York: Times Books, 1987), 313.

35. See Sale, 600–613 and Unger, 172–176.

36. Unger, 173.

37. Tom Thomas, "The Second Battle of Chicago 1969," in Jacobs, 201–203.

38. "The Left: Wild in the Streets," *Newsweek*, October 20, 1969, 44.

39. Thomas, 221–223.

40. Unger, 176.

41. Quoted in Thomas, 225.

42. Shin'ya Ono, "A Weatherman: You Do Need a Weatherman to Know Which Way the Wind Blows," in Jacobs, 271.

43. Ibid., 271–273.

44. Daniels, 439.

45. Unger, 177.

46. Sale, 613–614.

47. Unger, 176.

48. Nicholas Strinkowski, *The Organizational Behavior of Revolutionary Groups* (Ph.D. dissertation, Northwestern University, 1985), 84–85.

49. Quoted in Dellinger, p. 163.

50. Nigel Young, *An Infantile Disorder? The Crisis and Decline of the New Left* (Boulder, CO: Westview Press, 1977), 277.

51. Jacobs, 144.

52. Daniels, 440.

53. Sale, 629–630.

54. Unger, 181.

55. Quoted in Dellinger, p. 152.

56. Ibid., 166.

57. Ibid.

58. Sale, 628.

59. Collier and Horowitz, 95.

60. Ronald Fraser, *1968: A Student Generation in Revolt* (New York: Pantheon Books, 1988), p. 333.

61. This was the term the Weathermen used for their small, tightly organized cells scattered across the country. The affinity groups took orders from the organization's national leaders, called the Weather Bureau. In the absence of such orders, they carried out bomb attacks of their own. For an extended discussion of the Weathermen's organization while underground, see Strinkowski, 119–121 and 155–163.

62. Dellinger, 175.

63. Quoted in Morrison and Morrison, 319–320.

64. Dellinger, 175.

65. See, for example, Unger, 183.

66. Lawrence Lader, *Power on the Left* (New York: W. W. Norton, 1979), 304.

67. Dellinger, 153.

68. Strinkowski, 86.

69. "Communique #1 from the Weatherman Underground," in Jacobs, 510.

70. Strinkowski, 188.

71. Ibid., 262.

72. "Communique #4 from the Weatherman Underground," in Jacobs, 516.

73. Collier and Horowitz, 105.

74. Daniels, 443.

75. Quoted in Collier and Horowitz, 105. Note, however, that the phrase "military error" does not appear in all published versions of the statement. See Daniels, 444, note 53.

76. Quoted in Adelson, 248.

77. Dellinger, 174.

78. Collier and Horowitz, 112.

79. Strinkowski, 220.

80. Collier and Horowitz, 113.

81. Ibid., 113–114.

82. Ibid., 115–117.

83. Milton Cantor, *The Divided Left* (New York: Hill and Wang, 1978), 215.

84. Abe Peck, *Uncovering the Sixties* (New York: Pantheon Books, 1985), 229.

85. Daniels, 445.

86. Lader, 283.

87. Berhard K. Johnpoll and Lillian Johnpoll, *The Impossible Dream* (Westport, CT: Greenwood Press, 1981), 340.

88. Lader, 321.

89. Ralph Whitehead, "Weather Goes SDS?" *Commonweal* 91 (October 24, 1969): 92.

90. Marshall Berman, "Notes Toward a New Society," *Partisan Review* 38 (1971/72): 406.

91. Ono, 236.

92. Ibid., 242–43.

93. Gitlin, *The Sixties*, 393.

94. Dellinger, 171.

95. Adelson, 246.

96. Nancy Zaroulis and Gerald Sullivan, *Who Spoke Up?* (Garden City, NY: Doubleday, 1984), 314.

97. John Morton Blum, *Years of Discord* (New York: W. W. Norton, 1991), 364.

98. Unger, 183.

99. Miller, 295.

100. Young, 296.

101. Quoted in Zaroulis and Sullivan, 254.

Chapter Eight

While the Whole World Watched: Rhetorical Failures of Antiwar Protest*

The protest of some Americans against U.S. military involvement in Vietnam was undeniably significant. In terms of duration, intensity, and the number of people involved, the Vietnam War protest must be counted among the most important social upheavals of this century.[1]

Any public protest is essentially persuasive, and that directed against the war in Vietnam was no exception. The antiwar activists wanted American troops withdrawn from Southeast Asia, and they generally hoped to accomplish this goal by persuading the mass public that the war was morally wrong.[2] Earlier chapters demonstrated some of the ways they went about that task.

The conflict finally ended in 1975. American troops had been brought home two years earlier in response to public opinion, which had turned against the war; some commentators believe that antiwar protesters were largely responsible for that shift in support. Murray Polner contended that protest activities made "a serious dent on public opinion" about the war.[3] Former U.S. Senator Charles Goodell claimed that, as a result of protest activities, "public attitudes about the war shifted a bit further" in favor of American withdrawal.[4] Robert Nisbet argues that, but for antiwar protesters, the war "might well have continued much further into the future."[5] Nicholas von Hoffman asserted in 1975 that "the war would still be going on . . . had it not been for the protesting people in the streets."[6]

Every scientific study of public opinion regarding antiwar protest during the Vietnam period has come to essentially the same conclusion,

*Dan F. Hahn coauthored this chapter.

however: the protesters failed utterly to reduce mass public support for the Vietnam War. These findings may be discussed on three levels.

First, antiwar protest was not successful in persuading the mass public. William Berkowitz correlated fifteen significant antiwar demonstrations with public opinion polls taken during the period 1965–1971 and found no relationship between the protests and shifts in support away from the war.[7] E. M. Schreiber analyzed poll data and concluded that "there is no evidence that shows an effect of anti-Vietnam war demonstrations on reducing the American public's support for the war in Vietnam."[8]

Second, antiwar protesters were viewed negatively by the great majority of middle Americans. According to Howard Schuman, "Poll data show clearly that open protest against the war is not well regarded by the great majority of American adults."[9] Further support for this claim is provided by the Survey Research Center of the University of Michigan, which found in 1968 that almost 75 percent of Americans had essentially negative reactions to antiwar protesters.[10] According to Robert Lane and Michael Lerner, the National Opinion Research Center found in 1968 that approximately 10 percent of Americans supported the demonstrators at the Democratic National Convention that year, and that only about 25 percent of those respondents identifying themselves as "doves" (people favoring disengagement in Vietnam) disapproved of the violence used by the Chicago police in quelling the disturbance.[11]

Third, antiwar protesters probably increased support for the war by serving as a "negative reference group." When a cause is associated in the public mind with a group having negative connotations, the cause will also be evaluated in a negative way. Philip Converse, Warren Miller, Jerrold Rusk, and Arthur Wolfe concluded that those demonstrating against the war had become a negative reference group for the majority of Americans.[12] John Mueller showed how negative reference groups influenced public opinion during World War II and argued that "because their cause became associated with an extraordinarily unpopular reference group, any gain the opposition to the war in Vietnam may have achieved by forcefully bringing its point of view to public attention was nullified."[13] But others have contended that the effect of protest went beyond the nullification of possible gains. Both Schuman and W. L. Lunch and P. W. Sperlich maintained that antiwar protest caused many U.S. citizens to increase their support for the war effort because of their revulsion for the protesters.[14] As Gladys Ritchie claimed, "The American public was diverted from consideration of the issues behind student protest by the rage with which it responded to protest actions."[15]

Nor did protest have any significant effect on policymakers directly. Paul Burstein and William Frudenburg analyzed the impact of various factors, including demonstrations, on war-related votes in the U.S. Senate and concluded that the net effect of protest was nil. On the other hand, the senators did seem to respond to changes in public opinion and to the increasing costs of the war in money and lives.[16]

The executive branch also seemed unwilling to alter its course in response to protest. E. M. Schreiber found that "a review of accounts by participants [in the Johnson administration] and by journalists does not provide a basis for concluding that the Vietnam-related views of President Johnson or of his foreign policy advisors were changed by demonstrations."[17]

Of course, as history shows, public opposition to the war in Vietnam did gradually increase. But antiwar protest had little to do with this. Instead, the American public was responding to the failure of two administrations to win measurable victories, and to increasing American casualties. Schreiber determined that about 90 percent of the change in public opinion about the war could be explained by the length of the conflict and by U.S. losses.[18] Mueller found a direct correlation between the increase in American combat casualties and the increasing opposition to the war by middle America.[19] Further, one of the major reasons for Richard Nixon's high approval rating during his first term, and his landslide victory over George McGovern in the 1972 election, seemingly was his policy of "Vietnamization," which turned over more fighting to the South Vietnamese and thus decreased American losses.[20]

The public opinion data discussed hitherto show clearly that antiwar protesters did not succeed in persuading their fellow Americans to support an end to the fighting. But the opinion polls do not show *why* this occurred. The events of the Vietnam War era have faded too far into the past for further polling to be useful in exploring this issue.

The failure of the antiwar protesters to achieve their ultimate goals can be explored, however, by applying rhetorical principles to the acts of the protesters and the values of their audience. In the remainder of this chapter, we argue that the protesters' rhetorical failure had two main sources. We call the first of these the *intrinsic factors*; they relate to matters directly controlled by the protesters themselves. The other category involves audience variables, which were largely outside the protesters' control, but which nonetheless affected the way their message was received. These we call *extrinsic factors*. Taken together, the intrinsic and extrinsic factors show clearly why those who demonstrated against American involvement in Vietnam were not rhetorically effective.

INTRINSIC FACTORS

In writing about the Vietnam War era, a number of commentators have referred to "the antiwar movement." According to our understanding of the term, however, there was no such thing. Some of those who opposed the war did organize into groups, but others did not; some of the groups formed did last for a long time, but others were short-lived; some antiwar protesters were committed to long-term action, but others took part in only one or two demonstrations. We will thus not refer to an "antiwar movement" here but instead recognize that particular individuals and groups opposing the war made various choices as to the form and substance of their protest activities. Some of these choices, we believe, were rhetorically unsound. We will discuss six in particular: identification with the counterculture, immoderate protest tactics, the use of violence, attacks on capitalism, the use of obscenity, and desecration of the American flag. Not all protesters made all of these choices, or even any of them. But some protesters did—and, in the public mind, all were tarred with the same brush.[21]

Identification with the Counterculture

During the tumultuous decades of the 1960s and 1970s, the word "counterculture" was not unlike the word "hippie": it was often used imprecisely, broadly, and scathingly. It is possible, however, to approach an objective definition, the heart of which is contained in the word itself. Members of the counterculture espoused values that were often "counter" to the prevailing values of mainstream American "culture." A more detailed definition was offered by Lane and Lerner. The members of the counterculture, they wrote, "reject patriotism, respect for the police, puritan sexuality, the work-and-success ethic, consumerism, education as a social ladder, and, perhaps above all, the underlying presumption of Middle America that the American social order is a good and just one."[22]

The relationship between the counterculture and Vietnam War protesters was akin to that between chickens and eggs: precise cause and effect is difficult to determine. Prior to the significant commitment of troops to Vietnam, a number of persons had rejected traditional American values in favor of a less conventional lifestyle. The "beat generation" of the 1950s is a good example, and some of the "beatniks" became antiwar demonstrators a decade or more later. It is also clear, however, that America's increasing involvement in the Vietnam conflict, and the perceived willingness of the country's leaders to tolerate massive numbers of deaths, American and Vietnamese, in pursuit of political goals drove many young people away from middle America and into the counterculture.[23]

In retrospect, the manifestation of counterculture values by antiwar protesters through dress, grooming, slogans, public nudity, and drug use, among other things, was clearly a rhetorical error. The target audience for the antiwar protest, the citizens of middle America, found the antiwar protesters "distasteful, even threatening."[24] Theodore Windt pointed out that "each act [by counterculture protesters] seemed to backfire in the antiwar movement: each provided a rhetorical aid to supporters of the war, created an embarrassment to opponents of the war."[25] This realization led Lane and Lerner to conclude that "as long as the anti-war movement is identified with the counter-culture, its political power can scarcely increase."[26]

Opponents of the war made isolated efforts to avoid counterculture identification. As noted previously, during the 1968 New Hampshire primary, young supporters of antiwar presidential candidate Eugene McCarthy canvassed the state on his behalf. To avoid offending conservative New Hampshire voters, these volunteers agreed to "stay clean for Gene." They cut their hair, wore conventional clothing, and left illegal drugs back home. In the primary, McCarthy came in second to President Johnson by less than 300 votes, so perhaps the choice made by the senator's youthful supporters was the right one. Certainly, they seem not to have alienated large numbers of New Hampshire Democrats. But such audience adaptation by antiwar activists was the exception, not the rule.[27]

Immoderate Protest Tactics

The activities of opponents to the Vietnam War may be discussed in terms of a continuum of intensity. At one end were such mild actions as writing a letter to a senator or a newspaper, or voting for an antiwar candidate. In the middle, such behaviors as attending a rally against the war, giving a speech in a class or meeting, or circulating a petition might be found. At the other end of the continuum were more extreme activities. Many people who opposed the war never acted in an immoderate fashion—but some did.

Actually, the lack of moderation on the part of protesters may be discussed with respect to both *means* and *ends*. We will discuss immoderate ends first, and by these we mean the goals espoused by some protesters that were too extreme to appeal to the mass public. As Michael Mandelbaum points out, the goal proclaimed by many antiwar activists was "the immediate, unconditional withdrawal of American forces from Indochina."[28] This goal would be repugnant to most middle Americans for a long time for two reasons. First, many were loath to admit that those U.S. troops already dead had lost their lives in vain. The United States, it was widely believed, had never lost a war, and it would be cowardly to walk away from one now. The second reason that immediate withdrawal was a rhetorically unwise goal to urge is that it would have meant a Communist victory in Vietnam. Since anti-Communism runs strongly in the blood of many Americans, such a goal would have been rejected without consideration. We discuss this in greater detail under Extrinsic Factors.

The immoderate means to which some protesters resorted included activities that, although nonviolent, were often coercive, illegal, or both. Radical students harassed representatives of the Dow Chemical Company, which manufactured the napalm used in Vietnam, and military recruiters visiting campuses.[29] Some antiwar activists blockaded busy streets; others publicly burned their draft cards. Some radical Catholics, inspired by the activities of two priests, the Revs. Daniel and Philip Berrigan, adopted the protest tactic of raiding Selective Service offices and destroying the draft files contained there, either by burning (often with homemade napalm) or by pouring blood on them. These protesters, who became known in the press as the Catholic Left or the Catholic Ultra-Resistance, usually wanted to be arrested for their actions and later attempted to use their trials as propaganda forums from which to attack the war.[30]

The immoderate approaches to protest were almost guaranteed to alienate many members of middle America. Although it had become something of a cliche, it is nonetheless true to say that the average American believes in "law and order." This was as true during the Vietnam War as it is today. Those who disrupt the social order are likely to be viewed as outcasts and criminals. Whatever message they have to offer is unlikely to be received favorably.

Violence as a Protest Tactic

For some opponents of the war, the step from immoderate protest tactics such as those described above to outright violence was a short one. For example, members of the Students for a Democratic Society (SDS), frustrated by the ineffectiveness of years of peaceful protest, decided that their only chance to be heard lay with what were called "guerrilla tactics." As Ritchie noted:

The use of such tactics expressed the activist philosophy that the end justifies the means. Guerrilla tactics spoke of the SDS decision that all rules demanding rational discourse had been suspended, that the channels of communication had been blocked off, and that the speaker had as his intent the subjugation of an enemy.[31]

A splinter group of SDS, the Weather Underground, went furthest of all. The Weathermen concluded that peaceful protest was futile and that even the guerrilla tactics used the main SDS body were insufficient. They saw violent revolution as the only viable alternative. The result was disruption, bombing, and arson, along with other violent crimes.

It should be stressed that the Weathermen were a minority within SDS, and that even the guerrilla tactics advocated by some SDS members were shunned by many protesters in favor of strictly nonviolent activity. But the violence did take place, and it shocked and frightened average citizens, convincing many that all antiwar protesters were revolutionaries. Nancy Zaroulis and Gerald Sullivan observed that "the Eleventh Street [site of a Weathermen bomb factory that blew up] blast destroyed . . . any possibility that the anti-war movement would ever be perceived in the public mind as anything but mindlessly violent."[37]

Attacks on Capitalism

Some of those who opposed American involvement in Vietnam went beyond that concern to criticize the entire economic basis of American society. They saw the war as a natural extension of the forces that dominated and poisoned the entire culture; for them, the real enemy was capitalism. The attacks on the capitalist system took two forms: rhetoric and physical destruction. The rhetorical attack is typified by Mark Rudd, member of the Columbia University SDS chapter and prominent student radical. Rudd claimed that, although the United States is supposed to be a land of free competition, in fact most economic power is concentrated within a few corporate monopolies. He maintained that "those who control the monopolies exercise tremendous power on society both economically, through the production and capital of their corporations, and politically, through their ties with the government."[33]

Other antiwar protesters in addition to Mark Rudd saw capitalism as the greater evil behind the evil war, and some of them went so far as to conduct "raids" on corporate offices, where documents were destroyed and anticapitalist diatribes were issued as press releases. A group calling itself the "DC Nine" made such a raid on the Dow Chemical Company in 1969, and in a public statement condemned Dow "and all similar American corporations. . . . We are outraged by the death-dealing exploitation of the people of the Third World, and of all the poor and powerless who are victimized by your power-seeking ventures."[34] The office of General Electric's Washington lobbyists was the object of a similar invasion in 1970.

The lack of rhetorical sensitivity involved in these attacks, rhetorical and otherwise, on the economic system of this country is probably so obvious as not to require a great deal of discussion. Most Americans, whether they have grown rich under capitalism or not, have never doubted its essential value as a philosophy. Research by Robert Lane into the values held by middle-class citizens found a deep and abiding faith in capitalism, a faith that placed middle Americans on a collision course with those protesters who attacked the American system.[35] The protesters would be seen as crackpots, or, worse, Communists. Their words on all subjects would encounter deaf ears and closed minds.

Use of Obscenity

Many antiwar protesters, especially those engaged in demonstrations, used obscene communication. This included words and phrases widely regarded in this culture as obscene, making obscene gestures, often toward authority figures, such as police officers and university officials, and throwing containers full of urine or feces. Such activity may have seemed mindless to observers, but it did, in fact, serve some specific purposes for the protesters, even while helping to defeat their larger purpose. As Haig Bosmajian demonstrated, the use of obscenity by protesters can serve as a manifestation of the protesters' liberation from despised social constraints; allow the protesters to define their opponents (e.g., the "establishment," the government, the university administration, the police) in strongly negative terms, hence increasing determination to act against them; provoke overreaction from the authorities, which demonstrates the "establishment's" brutality and wins sympathy for the protesters; allow the venting of frustrations felt by the protesters; and allow the protesters to conceal their own anxieties and insecurities.[36]

But there are also significant disadvantages to the use of obscenity in protest, according to Charles Stewart, Craig Smith, and Robert Denton. One problem is that obscenity "tends to draw attention to itself" and away from the cause the protest represents. Further, because obscenity is the most intense form of verbal combat, the only possible escalation from that point involves actual physical violence, the disadvantages of which have already been discussed. Finally, and most important from a rhetorical perspective, the use of public obscenity alienates and disgusts many American citizens.[37] As J. D. Rothwell notes, although many middle Americans engage in obscene speech privately, they regard the public obscenity of demonstrators with great disapproval.[38] Bosmajian reports that many who observed the use of obscenity by antiwar protesters found them "repulsive, distasteful, and objectionable."[39] Windt concludes that the Vietnam-era protest group Youth International Party, whose members were known as Yippies, made a specialty of public obscenity and "alienated from their cause as many, if not more, than they drew to it."[40]

Desecration of the Flag

As we noted earlier, some antiwar protesters had concluded that the Vietnam conflict was only a symptom of a greater disease. They decided that America was essentially corrupt and evil; some even spelled the country's name "Amerika" to suggest fascist connotations. A relatively small number of demonstrators took out their distaste for the nation on its flag. During some antiwar demonstrations, the American flag was burned, torn to pieces, dragged through mud, or used as a toilet. A few protesters wore the flag sewn into an article of clothing, frequently the seat of the pants. This behavior constituted what Richard Goodman and William Gorden call "the rhetoric of desecration," and if the use of public obscenity by protesters was likely to shock and dismay members of the "silent majority," then desecration of the flag was guaranteed to enrage them. For most average citizens, the very people to whom the antiwar message was supposed to be directed, disrespect for the flag was seen as "intolerable, treasonous behavior."[41] Succinctly put, "to burn the flag of one's own nation is to become the enemy."[42] The essential error made by the protesters who engaged in flag desecration was a failure to see that one could oppose the war without necessarily being unpatriotic. They attacked the war by attacking, in fundamental ways, the nation waging it. As Jack Beatty concluded, "The great error of the left was to take out its anger at the war on the patriotic symbol that cloaked it."[43]

The result among middle Americans observing such behavior has been termed by Charles Elder and Roger Cobb "connotative overflow."[44] This means that symbols can become linked together in the minds of an audience, and when one symbol is evaluated in negative terms, the other symbols associated with it are also seen as negative. Observing that "it became commonplace for war protesters to attack the symbols of patriotism they associated with the war," Elder and Cobb concluded that "[r]egardless of their previous feelings toward the war, many Americans found such actions intolerable."[45] Desecration of the flag was connected in the public mind with antiwar protest, and the hatred and disgust inspired by the former spilled over into the latter.

The overall impact of what we have termed *intrinsic factors* was a great reduction in ethos for antiwar protesters with respect to their ultimate audience, middle-class Americans. The importance of ethos, or personal credibility, for any effort at persuasion has been widely documented. Aristotle wrote that the rhetor's character may almost be called the most effective means of persuasion he possesses. Modern experimental research supports this conclusion. Gerald Miller, Edward Wotring, and Elliot Siegel found that "research has consistently indicated that the greater the perceived credibility of the source, the more likely the receiver is to accept the source's influence attempts."[46] Michele Tolela Myers and Alvin Goldberg also concluded that source credibility was a major factor in the success of persuasion.[47]

The choices made by some antiwar protesters effectively destroyed the ethos of *all* antiwar protesters, as far as middle America was concerned. As we discussed previously, some protesters made choices that depicted values grossly at odds with those of the average citizen. One effect of these choices, such as attacking capitalism, using public obscenity, or desecrating the flag, was to emphasize the difference in values between the protesters and their middle-class audience. To a significant degree, credibility depends on perceived similarity between message source and audience. Herbert Simons, N. Berkowitz, and J. R. Moyer noted that "[c]ommunicators who are perceived as similar to their audience are more likely to effect persuasion than those sources who are seen as dissimilar."[48] Similar conclusions were reached by Dominic Infante[49] and Don Schweitzer.[50] The actions of some antiwar protesters had the effect of emphasizing differences, not similarities, between the protesters and their audience. The result was low ethos and failure to turn public opinion against the war.

It should be made clear, however, that there were reasons for the choices made by antiwar protesters, even if hindsight shows those choices to be ill-advised. We will discuss two of those reasons: (1) the lack of organization among opponents of the war and (2) the difficulty involved in motivating people to engage in moderate protest.

For those who opposed the Vietnam War, there was no single organization, no governing body to which all protesters were accountable, no generally acknowledged leader. As Jerome Skolnick pointed out at the height of the conflict over the war, "The peace movement does have some broad continuities and tendencies, well understood by the most important leaders, but . . . its loosely participatory, unstructured aspect can scarcely be overestimated."[51] Protest activities were performed by members of many organizations, both large and small, as well as by a host of small groups and individuals who acted more or less independently.

The result of this lack of organization has been described as a "cacophony of ideas, groups, and individuals" involved in protest against the war.[52] There was general agreement about the overall goal, which was "end the war and bring American troops home"[53]; but agreement existed about little else, including the choice of protest tactics. Those who wanted to write letters wrote them; those willing to march and demonstrate picked up their picket signs; those who were inclined toward violence prepared their bombs. Even if there were protest leaders perceptive enough to realize the adverse rhetorical effects of some forms of protest, they had little ability to control the actions of others.

Other protest leaders, even if personally inclined toward moderate protest activity, did not always encourage moderation in their followers. There were two reasons for this. The first was frustration. Opponents of the war had relied on essentially moderate tactics from about 1962 to 1966 and had failed to reverse, slow, or influence in any way American

military involvement in Vietnam.[54] Early protesters used mostly deco-
rous language and employed the traditional channels of communication
to send their antiwar messages. But policymakers ignored the messages,
and the old forms of protest, such as teach-ins, eventually grew trite.
Moderate protesters faced additional frustrations. As William Jurma
notes, moderates opposing the war had to respond "to being harassed
by target establishments, to being abandoned by their followers, to being
challenged by more militant protest groups, and to being dismissed by
the media."[55]

A second reason that some protest leaders abandoned moderation
was that it is difficult to energize people if the action desired is a moderate
one. As Herbert Simons points out, "Leaders of moderate groups frequently complain that their supporters are apathetic."[56] On the other
hand, strong commitment to a goal often manifests itself in the attitude
that any means are justified to achieve that goal. Thus, those most likely
to exert themselves on behalf of a cause are also the most prone to
employ immoderate tactics on the cause's behalf.

Even if there were a tightly organized antiwar "movement," however,
and even if those influential within it were disposed to counsel moderation in protest activity, there were a number of other reasons that
the protesters' message would not have been accepted by middle Americans. Because they were outside the direct control of the antiwar activists, we call these *extrinsic factors*.

EXTRINSIC FACTORS

Anti-Communism

Since the end of World War II, opposition to Communism has been
a major force in the United States. Although the McCarthy era of black-
lists, hysteria, and Congressional persecution occurred in the 1950s, anti-
Communist feeling was still strong during the Vietnam War. As Michael
Smith observed, "Conditioned by the Cold War rhetoric of the fifties
and early sixties, the American public shared an intense but generalized
hostility toward 'Communism' and all 'Communist' countries."[57] This
attitude was encouraged and exploited by presidents Kennedy, Johnson,
and Nixon, all of whom portrayed the Vietnam War as a struggle against
Communist domination of Southeast Asia.[58]

The effect of these anti-Communist appeals on public opinion was
predictable: most Americans wanted to defeat the Communists in Vietnam. A 1966 poll by the National Opinion Research Center found that
81 percent of those surveyed opposed U.S. withdrawal from Vietnam
because it would mean a Communist victory in that country.[59]

Such views made it difficult for opponents of the war to win the hearts and minds of their countrymen. If America did what the protesters wanted, which was to end the war, the Communists would win. That, for a long time, was unthinkable.

Opposition to Protest in Any Form

Historically, any nontraditional dissent with the status quo has been viewed with disfavor by most Americans. Indeed, this intolerance for any but the mildest forms of protest has been termed "a general characteristic of contemporary political culture in the United States."[60] Converse and Schuman concur, pointing out that the majority of Americans oppose any protest "that goes beyond the confines of conventional debate."[61] Data gathered in 1968 demonstrate this clearly. Fewer than 20 percent of those polled approved of people taking part in protest marches or demonstrations, even if these had been approved by local authorities.[62] Middle Americans do not like social protest, regardless of its subject. They are thus unlikely to be persuaded by it.

A related problem is the "contrast effect" that seems to operate with respect to protest demonstrations. Even peaceful acts of civil disobedience were often perceived as being far more threatening than they actually were, especially if other protesters had, on other occasions known to the audience, engaged in violence. As Michael Novak points out, "Whatever the private *intention* of their agents, public symbolic acts are necessarily interpreted according to the hermeneutics supplied by the cultural histories of which they are a part."[63] Bosmajian observes that certain acts of protest, such as desecration of the flag or the destruction of Selective Service records, although not designed to be part of a revolution, were nonetheless perceived that way by others.[64] Thus, even mildly unconventional protest was often seen by middle Americans as an attempt to rend the fabric of society.

Violence by Opponents of Protest

We have already noted that some antiwar protesters engaged in violence against property and persons. They were a small minority, but they gave notoriety to all protesters, even the most peaceful. Another factor contributing to the violent reputation of antiwar demonstrators was the violence inflicted *on* them by civil authorities, opponents of their cause, or both. The extended demonstration in Chicago during the 1968 Democratic National Convention is illustrative. Although many protesters in Chicago flagrantly provoked the police, using taunts, insults, and various forms of obscenity, it is generally agreed that most of the violence committed during the turbulent week came from the police themselves.[65] As we have already pointed out, however, most Americans watching the melee on their television screens blamed the violence on the demonstrators. The Task Force Report to the National Commission on the Causes and Prevention of Violence concluded:

While there have been scattered acts of real violence committed by anti-war activists, by far the greater portion of physical harm has been done *to* demonstrators and movement workers, in the form of bombings of homes and offices, crowd-control measures used by police, physical attacks on demonstrators by American Nazi Party members, Hell's Angels, and others. . . .
    Counterdemonstrators have repeatedly attacked and beaten peace marchers, sometimes with tacit police approval.[66]

Even though antiwar protesters did not typically initiate whatever violence might be associated with them, they had so thoroughly alienated middle America that the protesters usually received the blame for the violence that occurred.

Media Coverage

In a nation the size of the United States, any group with a national goal must have the attention of the news media to communicate its message widely. Certainly many Americans, especially those who did not live in large cities or near the campuses of universities, gained most of their information about antiwar protest during the Vietnam era from the news media. The effect of the media in this regard cannot be overstated. As Jurma points out, "Protest groups will not succeed if their tactics are not considered significant for media coverage. . . . The scope and tone of coverage affects subsequent actions of leaders and their followers, target establishments, and the public."[67] We will discuss media coverage of the antiwar protesters in three areas: extent, type, and tone.

The extent of news media coverage of antiwar protest varied somewhat over the course of the war, although it never reached a very high level. Prior to 1965, television coverage in particular was minimal. For example, a number of large demonstrations that took place during 1964 were virtually invisible as far as the national news media were concerned.[68] From 1965 to 1969, more stories about protest appeared, although such items were never preeminent among news stories. CBS News, for example, never devoted to antiwar demonstrations more than 20 percent of its total coverage of Vietnam-related stories.[69] Televised stories about demonstrations declined again from 1969. This was partly due to the winding down of the war by President Nixon, although the amount of protest did not significantly decline, and partly the result of a rhetorical assault on the news media by the White House, largely in the person of Vice President Spiro Agnew. As noted in Chapter 4, Agnew made a series of well-publicized speeches critical of the national media's fairness toward the president and his policies. Although high network executives publicly denied the charges and claimed the government was attempting to curb their First Amendment rights, there were, nonetheless, fewer stories focusing on antiwar protest following Agnew's diatribes.[70]

Not surprisingly, when stories about antiwar activity did appear, they tended to focus on the sensational. In their analysis of the rhetorical dimensions of news, Kathleen Hall Jamieson and Karlyn Kohrs Campbell posit five characteristics of news in American culture, three of which are especially relevant to this discussion. They are that "[h]ard news is dramatic, conflict-filled, and violent"; "[h]ard news is action, an event, an observable occurrence"; and "[h]ard news is novel, deviant, out of the ordinary."[71] It is natural, therefore, that reporters and editors would focus their attention on the aspects of antiwar protest that were violent, disruptive, and shocking. Prior to 1966, almost all antiwar protest was restrained and peaceful; as a result, hardly anyone in America who had not personally witnessed such protest was aware it had taken place. It was ignored by the news media. Later, as protesters became frustrated and turned to the immoderate tactics already discussed, they began to receive attention from the fourth estate. Todd Gitlin points out that "[t]he most outrageous, most discordant, most 'colorful' symbols were the surest to be broadcast—'Viet Cong' flags, burning draft cards and (later) flags and (still later) ROTC buildings."[72] Since most antiwar people were not stupid, they realized the dynamics of the situation and began to "play the game." They did what was necessary to attract the attention of the television cameras: they shouted, postured, chanted, gestured obscenely, disrupted, and were violent.[73]

The tone of the media coverage was also important. By "tone," we mean the overall impression created by a news story and by its juxtaposition with other news stories. Clearly, the tone of news stories about antiwar protest was usually negative. Rarely was protest depicted as an attempt to communicate a message; instead, the emphasis in news stories was on protest as social disruption.[74]

Frequently a story on U.S. troops fighting in Vietnam was juxtaposed with another story on antiwar protest at home. The implicit message communicated by the contrast seems to be clear: Americans protesting the war were giving "aid and comfort to the enemy," the same enemy that was killing U.S. soldiers in Vietnam.[75] Gitlin concluded that in the news media, opponents of the war were "surrounded by a firebreak of discrediting images."[76] The protesters did eventually succeed in attracting news coverage of their activities, but it was not the sort of coverage likely to advance their cause of persuading America to abandon the war.

Polarization by Political Figures

As we have shown, many antiwar protesters foolishly—from a rhetorical standpoint—attempted to distance themselves from the values and norms of middle America. This division was exacerbated by certain politicians during the Vietnam War, especially by President Nixon and Vice President Agnew. In what Andrew King and Floyd Anderson call "the rhetoric of polarization,"[77] Nixon attempted to heighten his identification with the "silent majority" by emphasizing the differences between the members of that group and stereotyped antiwar protesters.[78] During some of Nixon's speeches around the country, his representatives instructed local police to allow a small number of demonstrators entrance to the auditorium where the president was speaking. Predictably, the demonstrators would chant, often obscenely, and Nixon would work their protest into his speech, telling his predominantly middle-class audience, "Is that the voice of America? . . . I say to you it is not. . . . Answer in the powerful way that Americans have answered. . . . Speak up with your votes. That is the way to answer."[79]

Nixon portrayed himself and the Republican party as the defenders of traditional values and encouraged his audiences to view antiwar protesters as different from them—offensively different. In both the Congressional elections of 1970 and the national election two years later, Nixon and Agnew played this theme again and again, and their rhetoric of polarization probably contributed to the Republican successes in those contests.[80] It is likely that their tactics helped to convince middle Americans that the antiwar protesters, and their message urging peace, must be rejected.

CONCLUSION

Although antiwar protesters, taken as a group, were a heterogeneous lot, they nonetheless had one overall goal: "To persuade the American public that [the Vietnam War] ought to be stopped."[81] Although some commentators, noting that the war *did* stop, have claimed a victory for the war's opponents, analysis of the dynamics of public opinion during the period shows just the opposite. The American public rejected the antiwar protesters' argument that the war was immoral and unjustified; middle America became disenchanted only when the oft-promised victory in Vietnam proved elusive and the casualties began to mount. In many respects, the antiwar protesters were their own worst enemies. They made choices to satisfy themselves or to achieve short-run goals. The ultimate goal of mass persuasion was often forgotten. As Converse et al. concluded about the war's opponents, "There was simply no comprehension of the dynamics of public opinion at all."[82]

But even if the demonstrators had been unified under a leader or leaders who were able to make and enforce sound rhetorical choices, the row to hoe would have been a hard one. Average Americans of the 1960s and 1970s were suspicious of protest, generally supportive of presidential actions, and very concerned about Communism. Even if all the antiwar protesters had dressed and groomed themselves conventionally, spoken and marched with decorum, and acted with self-restraint in public, the prevailing attitudes of the mass public would have provided formidable obstacles on the path to peace.

NOTES

1. William R. Berkowitz, "The Impact of Anti-Vietnam Demonstrations upon National Public Opinion and Military Indicators," *Social Science Research* 2 (1973): 3.

2. E. M. Schreiber, "Anti-war Demonstrations and American Public Opinion on the War in Vietnam," *British Journal of Sociology* 27 (1976): 225.

3. Murray Polner, *No Victory Parades: The Return of the Vietnam Veteran* (New York: Holt, Rinehart and Winston, 1971), 151.

4. Charles Goodell, *Political Prisoners in America* (New York: Random House, 1973), 141.

5. Robert Nisbet, "Who Killed the Student Revolution?" *Encounter* (February 1970): 16.

6. Nicholas von Hoffman, "Good Soldiers Don't Ask Why," *The Washington Post*, May 2, 1975, B8.

7. Berkowitz, 10.

8. Schreiber, 232.

9. Howard Schuman, "Two Sources of Anti-War Sentiment in America," *American Journal of Sociology* 78 (1972): 516.

10. Philip E. Converse and Howard Schuman, " 'Silent Majorities' and the Vietnam War," *Scientific American* (June 1970), 23.

11. Robert E. Lane and Michael Lerner, "Why Hard-Hats Hate Hairs," *Psychology Today*, November 1970, 45.

12. Philip E. Converse, Warren E. Miller, Jerrold G. Rusk, and Arthur C. Wolfe, "Continuity and Change in American Politics: Parties and Issues in the 1968 Election," *American Political Science Review* 63 (1969): 1105.

13. John E. Mueller, *War, Presidents, and Public Opinion* (New York: John Wiley & Sons, 1973), 165.

14. Schuman, p. 517; W. L. Lunch and P. W. Sperlich, "American Public Opinion and the War in Vietnam," *Western Political Quarterly* 32 (1979): 31.

15. Gladys Ritchie, "Youth Rebels: A Decade of Protest," in *America in Controversy*, ed. D. Holland (Dubuque, IA: Wm. C. Brown, 1973), 408.

16. Paul Burstein and William Freudenburg, "Changing Public Policy: The Impact of Public Opinion, Anti-war Demonstrations, and War Costs on Senate Voting on Vietnam War Motions," *American Journal of Sociology* 84 (1978): 116.

17. E. M. Schreiber, "American Politics and the Vietnam Issue: Demonstrations, Votes, and Public Opinion," *Politics* 10 (1975): 207.

18. Schreiber, "American Politics and the Vietnam Issue: Demonstrations, Votes, and Public Opinion," 207.

19. John E. Mueller, "Trends in Popular Support for the Wars in Korea and Vietnam," *American Political Science Review* 65 (1971): 366.

20. Daniel C. Hallin, *The "Uncensored War"* (New York: Oxford University Press, 1986), 182.

21. Converse, Miller, Rusk, and Wolfe, 1105.

22. Lane and Lerner, 46.

23. John Hellman, *American Myth and the Legacy of Vietnam* (New York: Columbia University Press, 1986), 75.

24. Michael Mandelbaum, "Vietnam: The Television War," *Daedalus* 111 (1982): 166.

25. Theodore O. Windt, Jr., "The Diatribe: Last Resort for Protest," *Quarterly Journal of Speech* 58 (1972): 3.

26. Lane and Lerner, 45.

27. Randall M. Fisher, *Rhetoric and American Democracy* (Lanham, MD: University Press of America, 1985), 190.

28. Mandelbaum, 166.

29. Fisher, 191.

30. J. Justin Gustainis, "The Catholic Ultra-Resistance: Rhetorical Strategies of Anti-war Protest," *The Communicator* 13 (1983): 37–50.

31. Ritchie, 422.

32. Nancy Zaroulis and Gerald Sullivan, *Who Spoke Up?* (New York: Doubleday, 1984), 313.

33. Mark Rudd, "Columbia's Strike Leader: 'We Want Revolution,' " in *Perspectives for the 70s*, ed. R. G. Noreen and W. Graffin (New York: Dodd, Mead, 1971), 39–40.

34. Michael Ferber and Staughton Lynd, *The Resistance* (Boston: Beacon Press, 1971), 209–210.

35. Lane and Lerner, 36–37.

36. Haig A. Bosmajian, "Obscenity and Protest," *Today's Speech* 18 (1970): 11–13.

37. Charles Stewart, Craig Smith, and Robert E. Denton, *Persuasion and Social Movements* (Prospect Heights, IL: Waveland Press, 1984), 194–196.

38. J. D. Rothwell, "Verbal Obscenity: Time for Second Thoughts," *Western Speech* 35 (1971): 231–242.

39. Bosmajian, 9.

40. Windt, 14.

41. Richard J. Goodman and William I. Gorden, "The Rhetoric of Desecration," *Quarterly Journal of Speech* 57 (1971): 23.

42. Goodman and Gorden, 30.

43. Jack Beatty, "The Patriotism of Values," *The New Republic* (July 4–11, 1981), 19.

44. Charles D. Elder and Roger W. Cobb, *The Political Uses of Symbols* (New York: Longman, 1983), 77.

45. Elder and Cobb, 78.

46. Gerald Miller, C. Edward Wotring, and Elliot R. Siegel, "Source Credibility

and Credibility Proneness: A New Relationship," *Speech Monographs* 36 (1969): 118.

47. Michele Tolela Myers and Alvin A. Goldberg, "Group Credibility and Opinion Change," *Journal of Communication* 20 (1970): 174–179.

48. Herbert W. Simons, N. Berkowitz, and J. R. Moyer, "Similarity, Credibility, and Attitude Change," *Psychology Bulletin* 74 (1970): 1.

49. Dominic A. Infante, "The Function of Perceptions of Consequences in Attitude Formation and Communication Image Formation," *Central States Speech Journal* 23 (1972): 180.

50. Don A. Schweitzer, "The Effect of Presentation on Source Evaluation," *Quarterly Journal of Speech* 56 (1970): 39.

51. Jerome H. Skolnick, *The Politics of Protest* (New York: Simon and Schuster, 1969), 30.

52. Gabriel Kolko, *Anatomy of a War* (New York: Pantheon, 1985), 173.

53. Jess Yoder, "The Peace Movement and the Vietnam War," in *America in Controversy*, ed. DeWitt Holland (Dubuque, IA: Wm. C. Brown, 1973), 448.

54. Ritchie, 421.

55. William E. Jurma, "Moderate Movement Leadership and the Vietnam Moratorium Committee," *Quarterly Journal of Speech* 68 (1982): 272.

56. Herbert W. Simons, *Persuasion: Understanding, Practice, and Analysis*, rev. ed. (New York: Random House, 1986), 270.

57. F. Michael Smith, "Rhetorical Implications of the 'Aggression' Thesis in the Johnson Administration's Vietnam Argumentation," *Central States Speech Journal* 23 (1972): 222.

58. F. M. Kail, *What Washington Said* (New York: Harper & Row, 1973), 34; Cal M. Logue and John H. Patton, "From Ambiguity to Dogma: The Rhetorical Symbols of Lyndon B. Johnson on Vietnam," *Southern Speech Communication Journal* 47 (1982): 166; Robert P. Newman, "Under the Veneer: Nixon's Vietnam Speech of November 3, 1969," *Quarterly Journal of Speech* 56 (1970): 170.

59. Godfrey Hodgson, *America in Our Time* (Garden City, NY: Doubleday, 1976), 386.

60. Hallin, 196.

61. Converse and Schuman, 24.

62. Converse, et al., 1105.

63. Michael Novak, "Blue-bleak Embers . . . Fall, Gall Themselves . . . Gash Gold-Vermillion," in *Conspiracy: The Implications of the Harrisburg Trial for the Democratic Tradition*, ed. John C. Raines (New York: Harper & Row, 1974), 44.

64. Haig A. Bosmajian, "Introduction," in *Dissent; Symbolic Behavior and Rhetorical Strategies*, ed. Haig A. Bosmajian (Boston: Allyn and Bacon, 1972), 4.

65. Zaroulis and Sullivan, 194.

66. Skolnick, 66–67.

67. Jurma, 264.

68. J. Fred MacDonald, *Television and the Red Menace* (New York: Praeger, 1985), 69.

69. Hallin, 192.

70. Hodgson, 382.

71. Kathleen Hall Jamieson and Karlyn Kohrs Campbell, *The Interplay of Influence* (Belmont, CA: Wadsworth, 1983), 20–22.

72. Todd Gitlin, *The Whole World Is Watching* (Berkeley, CA: University of California Press, 1980), 182.

73. Hallin, 192.

74. Ibid., 199.

75. Ibid., 194.

76. Gitlin, 183.

77. Andrew A. King and Floyd A. Anderson, "Nixon, Agnew, and the 'Silent Majority': A Case Study in the Rhetoric of Polarization," *Western Speech* 35 (1971): 243.

78. Newman, 172.

79. Quoted in King and Anderson, 253.

80. Mandelbaum, 166.

81. Ibid., 164.

82. Converse, et al., 1105.

Part Three

The Rhetoric of the Media

Chapter Nine

B. D. Goes to 'Nam: *Doonesbury* as Antiwar Rhetoric

The idea that Garry Trudeau's comic strip *Doonesbury* contains rhetorical elements should come as no surprise to any student of contemporary American popular culture. The strip did, after all, win the 1975 Pulitzer Prize for editorial cartooning, and the rhetorical dimensions of editorial cartoons have been well documented by other scholars.[1]

One topic receiving recurring treatment in Trudeau's work was the Vietnam War. I contend that Trudeau consistently took an antiwar stance in *Doonesbury*, and that his antiwar rhetoric can be understood by examining two aspects of the comic strip: his depictions of American positions on the war and of Vietnamese positions. The plural form of "depiction" is used deliberately because Trudeau looks at both the American and Vietnamese positions from two aspects.

The two American positions on the war that Trudeau considers in his strip are the prowar and the antiwar positions. Each side will be examined here in two ways: through the use of characterization and through what might be called Trudeau's use of a "topper."

Consider first the prowar position. Various prowar perspectives are from time to time brought up in *Doonesbury*, but they are always assigned to unsympathetic characters. The two most commonly used unsympathetic characters are B. D. and President Richard Nixon.

Quarterback B. D., the strip's resident reactionary, is one of only two (along with Uncle Duke) recurring unsympathetic fictional characters in the strip (as opposed to Richard Nixon and Henry Kissinger, who were recurring, unsympathetic *nonfictional* characters). When Trudeau needed a prowar remark from among his regular characters, B. D. usually carried the ball—or dropped it, as the case may be. As *Time* magazine noted, "Trudeau was clearly appalled by the U.S. devastation of South-east Asia; but football-helmeted B. D. was given plenty of space to ra-tionalize."[2] But "rationalize" is not the best term to describe the role played by B. D. in Trudeau's antiwar rhetoric. "Putting his foot in his mouth" might be closer to the mark. B. D. delivered such howlers as "If you're going to fight Commies, you need eleven men on the field,"[3] "But this war had such promise,"[4] "But they're not [bombing those schools and hospitals] on purpose!"[5] and the immortal "The President is a lot smarter than you think!"[6]

It must be admitted that the issue of B. D. as an unsympathetic char-acter leads to a chicken-and-egg question. Does B. D. get those lines because he is unsympathetic, or is he unsympathetic because he spouts such lines? The former position seems more reasonable, if only because B. D. had been given many other occasions to establish his churlishness before the war in Vietnam became an issue in *Doonesbury*. He was already established as unsympathetic before he began to serve as a scapegoat for Trudeau's antiwar views.

The other unsympathetic *Doonesbury* character spouting prowar rhet-oric is President Nixon. Although the reader never sees Nixon's face (American presidents are never shown directly in *Doonesbury*—their dia-logue emanates either from a television being watched by one of the strip's regular characters, or from a building, such as the White House), the president is always clearly identified, and he has various prowar lines. In one strip, Nixon is depicted as saying,

Recently, as you know, Congress has been trying to pressure me into a dis-honorable peace in Vietnam. Well, I will not and cannot bow to this pressure. I don't care what Congress says, I'm sticking to my guns!! . . . Er, ah . . . I mean principles! . . . Sticking to my principles![7]

In another strip, the president is on television delivering a calm, mea-sured address about how he is winding down the war. Then, apparently, long-held frustration on his part boils over, and he says, "So kindly get off my back," and continues, shouting, "Do you hear me, you dumb peace freaks? Bug off, do you hear me? Just bug off!"[8]

On many earlier occasions in the strip, Trudeau had depicted Nixon negatively, as racist, insensitive, and stupid. So, although the same chicken-and-egg argument applicable to B. D. may be made here, and may even be stronger, since Nixon had an identity outside the strip and B. D. had none, a strong case can nonetheless be made for the claim that Trudeau was again assigning prowar statements to a character whom he had already shown to be unsympathetic.

Another way to look at prowar rhetoric in *Doonesbury* is to note that a "topper" usually follows prowar statements made by characters in the strip. The term "topper" (as in "Can you top this?") refers here to a response made by another character to "put down" or show the absurdity of prowar statements. Since, as noted, B. D. is the most frequent voice of sentiments supportive of the war, he is "topped" quite often by other characters in the strip. In one instance, he is reading a draft of one of his prowar term papers to a professor over the telephone, saying, "It is my belief that Lyndon Johnson will be remembered as one of the great ones. At a time when the war was at its most unpopular, Mr. Johnson showed courage, audacity and great leadership. It would be difficult not to compare him with Roger Staubach." In response, the professor counsels, "Try, B. D., try!"[9] On another occasion, B. D. is confronted by one of his football teammates with the accusation that the U.S. Air Force has been bombing civilian targets in North Vietnam, such as schools, dikes and hospitals. B. D. screams back, "But they're not doing it on *purpose!*" To this his teammate, Zonker, responds, naively, "Oh. . . . Well, that's different."[10]

By way of contrast, consider this example of a topper that is atypical of *Doonesbury* in two ways. First, the person doing the topping is that unlikely wit, Mike Doonesbury. Mike is usually the butt of other people's witticisms, but in this case he gets to deliver his own zinger. The second difference is that the person topped is none other than conservative political columnist Joseph Alsop, who is actually pictured in the strip. In Washington, Mike manages to go to a cocktail party for the elite and corners Alsop with a question about the war. Alsop replies, "Boy, it is a fact that we now see light at the end of the tunnel." Mike says, "No disrespect intended, sir, but when you've dug yourself into a hole, why do you always insist on calling it a 'tunnel.' " Even Alsop has to admit he has been topped. After a panel of silence, he says to Mike, "Touché, you little monster."[11]

Thus, when prowar statements appear in *Doonesbury*, they almost always come from the lips of a character previously shown to be unsympathetic. Further, such statements are frequently subjected to a topper by another character, a technique that makes the prowar statements appear foolish, if not downright absurd.

As might be imagined, Trudeau's treatment of the American antiwar position is somewhat different. For one thing, antiwar statements in *Doonesbury* are always given by sympathetic characters, with one exception, to be discussed later. Most of the antiwar messages come from such characters as Mike,[12] Mark Slackmeyer,[13] and even, on one memorable occasion, B. D.'s girlfriend, Boopsie, who is outraged by reports that the American bombing of North Vietnam has resulted in the slaughter of baby ducks.[14] No character who utters an antiwar statement is subjected to topping from another character.

But this is not to suggest that Garry Trudeau is entirely kind to opponents of the Vietnam War. The biggest problem with antiwar people, he seems to say in his strip, is that they are prone to getting wrapped up in their own clichés and have a tendency toward self-aggrandizement.

The cliché issue is best illustrated by a motif that Trudeau uses on two different occasions—one while the war is still in progress, the other shortly after the American withdrawal. The motif involves Mark Slack-meyer and his job as a campus disk jockey. In two strips published during the Vietnam War, Mark plays an on-the-air game, "Vietnam Quick Quiz." In the first strip, he asks his listening audience to guess how many tons of bombs were dropped on Vietnam during November 1972.[15] In the second, he asks, "What has been the effect of the war on the moral fiber of the nation?" A twelve-year-old girl calls in with the correct answer to the latter, which Mark jubilantly repeats on the air: "A deterioration of spiritual priorities is correct! You are today's WBBY winner!"[16] Both times, after announcing that the question has been answered correctly, Mark plays a prerecorded tape that proclaims, "We've got a winner!"

This motif appeared again shortly after the war was over. This time, Mark and Mike Doonesbury are on the radio together, conducting what they call an "Indochina Autopsy."[17] And, again, it is nothing more than a quiz show. Between commercials for pimple cream, the boys ask such questions as "Who is really to blame for the war?" " 'All of us' is right!" Mark exclaims, playing the "We've got a winner" tape again.[18]

Garry Trudeau does not seem to be making fun of people who opposed the war in Vietnam. Rather, he seems to be saying that much antiwar rhetoric had degenerated into mindless catchphrases that had ceased to have real meaning because people had stopped thinking about them. As a result, he says, many important issues had become nothing more than trivia in the minds of many, having about as much importance as the name of Roy Rogers' horse. Trudeau is not trying to trivialize the Vietnam War; rather, he is trying to show that many of the war's opponents have trivialized their own ideas.

The tendency for self-aggrandizement exhibited by some antiwar leaders is also a target for Trudeau's pen, and it is the one instance when an unsympathetic character is given antiwar lines to say. A series of three strips appearing in 1973 featured a Vietnam veteran named John Kerry, a real person, who is today a U.S. Senator from Massachusetts, who had become active against the war. Although one of the three strips serves as another occasion for B. D. to put his foot in his mouth (asking Kerry at an antiwar rally, "How can you moralize after throwing all your medals on the Capitol steps last Spring! Do you have any idea how much those medals cost the government?"),[19] the others depict Kerry as a self-centered egotist. In one, a man comes upon Mike and B. D., who are looking at a poster advertising the rally at which Kerry is scheduled to speak. He advises the boys, "If you care about this country at all, you better go listen to that John Kerry fellow. He speaks with a rare eloquence and astonishing conviction. If you see no one else this year, you must see John Kerry." After the man leaves, B. D. asks, "Who was that?" and Mike responds, deadpan, "John Kerry."[20] In the next strip, Kerry is speaking at the rally. He galvanizes the crowd with the line, "As far as the President's concerned, Vietnam means not having to say you're sorry!!" Basking in the ovation that follows, Kerry thinks to himself, "You're really clicking tonight, you gorgeous preppy."[21]

Obviously, Kerry is meant to be seen as a man whose need for ego gratification is much more important than his desire to speak out against the war. Trudeau does not mock what Kerry has to *say*, except for the "never having to say you're sorry" line, which is another excursion into cliché by an antiwar type, but he mocks Kerry himself. He is, in some respects, the liberal counterpart of B. D., although arguably more intelligent and eloquent.

The foregoing summarizes Trudeau's depiction of the American side of the Vietnam War, in terms of both its supporters and opponents. Another aspect to the war that was also grist for Trudeau's mill: the Vietnamese side. Again, Trudeau provides two views: one depicting the Viet Cong, the other focusing on the common people of Southeast Asia.[22]

The Viet Cong are mostly seen in the person of Phred, a young man in black pajamas who captures B. D. during his brief tour of duty in Vietnam but later sets him free. As *Time* inquired rhetorically, "Who else but Trudeau could have made an attractive character out of a Viet Cong terrorist?"[23] And therein lies the most important rhetorical aspect of this character. Phred is, by and large, sympathetic. In fact, back home in the states, even B. D. is forced to admit,

Phred's different from most of them [Communist] types. He often drinks beer, and he likes Chuck Berry records. And while I detest his politics, you gotta admire his dedication. He's been working for the V.C. for a long time! Phred's no Commie-come lately, you know![24]

This is not to suggest that Phred is without his dark side. He has one, and occasionally the reader catches glimpses of it. Lacking money to buy weapons, Phred tries to secure a grant from the Phord Foundation. When a member of the board asks Phred about the intended purpose of the grant, he responds, "My goal is to violently disrupt the social structure of Vietnamese society, thereby making it more receptive to a forced ideology." The board member says, "You mean 'Vietnamization,' of course." Phred replies, "I won't quibble."[25] Later, when filling out his grant application, Phred is asked to give a title to the proposed project. He calls it, "The Visceral Response of the Agrarian Southeast Asian to the Introduction of Sustained Automatic Weapons Fire."[26]

So, it would seem, Garry Trudeau is not rooting for the Viet Cong. Although Phred is portrayed as a nice person most of the time, he *is* a terrorist. He calls himself by that name, and he refers to acts of terrorism (although Trudeau never shows him committing any). If Trudeau is rooting for anyone in his comic strip, it is the common people of Southeast Asia, the innocent victims of the war.

An early manifestation of this occurs when Phred, who has been assigned to duty with the Pathet Lao, first enters Laos. A few refugees come upon him while he is cooking dinner and say, "We have not eaten in days! Could not some of us share in the hot rice dinner you have prepared for yourself?" Phred agrees to share his food, and asks, "How many of you are there?" The refugee responds, "135,000."[27]

Later, Phred journeys to Cambodia for a vacation, in the hope of being able to witness the anticipated Communist takeover of that country. Cambodia had been touted to him as a prime vacation spot, full of quaint temples for the tourist to visit. But when Phred arrives, the country has been devastated. He comes on the ruins of a temple and asks its peasant curator if the place was destroyed during the secret bombings carried out by the U.S. Air Force. The peasant responds, "Secret bombings? Boy, there wasn't any *secret* about them. Everyone here knew!"[28]

Shortly thereafter, Phred arrives at what may be the world's largest refugee camp, which contains more than 300,000 victims of the war.[29] Although there is humor to be found in Trudeau's depiction of the camp (Phred organizes a delegation to go to Washington and protest the situation to the U.S. Congress—a delegation that is to be smuggled into America hidden in crates marked "Coca-Cola"), there is a strong underlying tone of sadness and pity.

Trudeau's argument seems to be that the Americans in Southeast Asia are wrong, and that the Viet Cong and other revolutionary movements are wrong, too. They all have their axes to grind, and the peasants are ground up between them.

Thus, the case can be made that much of Garry Trudeau's depiction of the Vietnam War in *Doonesbury* may be seen as antiwar rhetoric. He is not a supporter of the American position; he is not a supporter of the Viet Cong position. He is, in his comic strip, a supporter of the common people, those who are always the primary victims of war.

NOTES

1. With respect to the rhetorical aspects of editorial cartoons, see Matthew C. Morrison, "The Role of the Political Cartoonist in Image Making," *Central States Speech Journal* 20 (1969): 252–260; see also Martin J. Medhurst and Michael

A. Desousa, "Political Cartoons as Rhetorical Form: A Taxonomy of Graphic Discourse," *Communication Monographs* 48 (1981): 197–236. Regarding the rhetorical dimensions of comic strips, see Kathleen J. Turner, "Comic Strips: A Rhetorical Perspective," *Central States Speech Journal* 28 (Spring 1977): 24–35.

2. "Doonesbury: Drawing and Quartering for Fun and Profit," *Time*, February 9, 1976, 65.

3. G. B. Trudeau, *Still a Few Bugs in the System* (New York: Holt, Rinehart and Winston, 1972), 17. The *Doonesbury* daily comic strips periodically appear in trade paperback editions, and the cartoons cited in this essay were taken from these collections. Pages in these editions are not numbered; I have therefore taken the liberty of employing my own numbering system. The first cartoon to appear in each book (they appear one to a page) was numbered page 1, and all the others that followed were numbered in sequence accordingly. Thus, the reference to "17" above refers to the seventeenth cartoon page in that book.

4. This quotation is the title of one of the *Doonesbury* paperback collections.

5. G. B. Trudeau, *Call Me When You Find America* (New York: Holt, Rinehart and Winston, 1973), 87.

6. G. B. Trudeau, *The President Is a Lot Smarter Than You Think* (New York: Holt, Rinehart and Winston, 1973), 16.

7. Ibid., 45.

8. *Still a Few Bugs in the System*, 82.

9. G. B. Trudeau, *Guilty, Guilty, Guilty!* (New York: Holt, Rinehart and Winston, 1974), 35.

10. *Call Me When You Find America*, 87.

11. *Still a Few Bugs in the System*, 110.

12. G. B. Trudeau, *"Speaking of Inalienable Rights, Amy. . . ."* (New York: Holt, Rinehart and Winston, 1976), 89.

13. *The President Is a Lot Smarter Than You Think*, 55.

14. *Call Me When You Find America*, 85.

15. *Guilty, Guilty, Guilty!* 28.

16. Ibid., 29.

17. *"Speaking of Inalienable Rights, Amy. . . ."* 89.

18. Ibid., 90.

19. *The President Is a Lot Smarter Than You Think*, 88.

20. Ibid., 86.

21. Ibid., 87.

22. The term "Southeast Asia" is used here, rather than "Vietnam," because some of the strips considered involve activities in Laos and Cambodia.

23. "Doonesbury: Drawing and Quartering for Fun and Profit," 65.

24. *Call Me When You Find America*, 105.

25. G. B. Trudeau, *Wouldn't a Gremlin Have Been More Sensible?* (New York: Holt, Rinehart and Winston, 1975), 60.

26. Ibid., 70.

27. *Guilty, Guilty, Guilty!* 83.

28. G. B. Trudeau, *"What Do We Have for the Witnesses, Johnnie?"* (New York: Holt, Rinehart and Winston, 1975), 92.

29. Ibid., 95.

Chapter Ten

From Savior to Psycho and Back Again: The Changing Role of Green Berets in Vietnam Films

All nations have their heroic legends and literature; the United States is no exception. Dan Nimmo and James Combs refer to a fundamental part of American culture that they call the "American monomyth." This refers to an account of a pure, brave, dedicated, American hero who defeats evildoers by virtue of his superior skills and high moral purpose.[1] One of the most prominent manifestations of the American monomyth is the Frontier Hero.

It naturally follows that the Frontier Hero is often seen in the garb of the Western cowboy. Televised frontier heroes were often cowboys, and they all fit the mold; they were physically tough heroic figures able to use the technology available to defeat their enemies.[2] But the Frontier Hero is not exclusive to Westerns. He has assumed many guises in modern American culture—even, on occasion, the role of the business executive who must show courage and endure great hardship on the road to corporate success.[3]

When the focus shifts from Southwestern prairies and urban boardrooms to the jungles of Vietnam, however, the mantle of the Frontier Hero is worn by the U.S. Army Special Forces, popularly known as the Green Berets. John Hellman characterizes the Special Forces trooper as the "contemporary reincarnation of the western hero,"[4] and Alasdair Spark concurs, saying that

the Green Beret has proved a consistent focus for popular interest in the Vietnam War. Alone of all the many U.S. Army and Marine units to see service in the war, the Green Berets secured and have sustained a place in the popular imagination. From the very beginnings of American involvement, through withdrawal to post-war self-examination, the myth of the Green Beret has served as a vehicle to express the purpose and experience of Vietnam.[5]

The Green Beret myth has been played out in a variety of ways and places: in newspapers and magazine reports, in presidential rhetoric, in Robin Moore's collection of short stories, *The Green Berets*, and in films. As Leo Cawley noted, "In Vietnam movies across the political spectrum, the American martial spirit is embodied either in the grunt or in the Special Forces soldier."[6] A number of films have used the Green Beret figure to express viewpoints about the Vietnam War, but those viewpoints have differed in interesting ways. This chapter examines four well-known Vietnam War films—*The Green Berets*, *The Deer Hunter*, *Apocalypse Now*, and *Rambo: First Blood Part II*—and shows how varying depictions of Green Berets have been used to make statements about the war itself.

GREEN BEANIE AS COWBOY HAT: THE DUKE WINS THE WAR

The 1968 film *The Green Berets*, based loosely on Robin Moore's book of the same name, featured John Wayne as producer, director, and star. It was the first film to address the war explicitly. Other filmmakers, desiring to have their movies appeal to the widest possible audience, shied away from the Vietnam War as a subject; they recognized that no film about the war could possibly be neutral, and that any such film would be bound to offend many Americans of one political persuasion or another. But John Wayne was willing to embrace controversy, believing that "it is extremely important that not only the people of the U.S., but people all over the world, should know why it is necessary for us to be in Vietnam."[7]

Wayne's views were thus consistent with the Johnson administration's Vietnam policy, and his film has been called an "unabashed tribute" to that policy.[8] It is not surprising that the film was made with the cooperation of the Defense Department. The Pentagon spent more than $1 million in loaned equipment and man hours on *The Green Berets*, of which Wayne was billed about $18,000.[9] In return, the government was able to alter the script substantially. The result has been called "blatant hawk propaganda for the Vietnamese war."[10]

The heroic nature of Special Forces soldiers is never in doubt throughout the film. In the early scenes at the Special Warfare School in Fort Bragg, North Carolina, the Green Berets demonstrate their skills in unarmed combat, demolitions, marksmanship, and foreign languages. Later, in Vietnam, the men are as heroic as one could wish. They fight courageously, counsel wisely, and, if necessary, die bravely. The overall message seems to be that when it comes to the war, "Trust the judgment of the Green Berets; the elite fellowship 'in the field' knows best."[11]

Despite considerable political controversy, the film made money: it was one of the most popular films in 1968. But title and subject matter notwithstanding, *The Green Berets* is not really a Vietnam War film. It might be considered, on the one hand, to be "an old-fashioned, patriotic pro-war film that could just as well have been about World War II."[12] On the other hand, *mutatis mutandis*, it is a typical John Wayne Western, a Manichean struggle between "good" cowboys and "bad" Indians, with innocent settlers caught in the middle. Substitute the words "Green Berets," "Viet Cong," and "South Vietnamese" for "cowboys," "Indians," and "settlers" in the preceding sentence, and the meaning becomes clear. But *The Green Berets* is not a complex film, and its rhetorical vision does not lend itself to complex analysis.

THE GREEN BERET AS DAMAGED HERO

John Wayne's simplistic portrayal of Green Beret heroics was superseded by other Vietnam films, in particular *The Deer Hunter* and *Apocalypse Now*. *The Deer Hunter* is not usually regarded as a "Green Beret film," but the Special Forces play an important role in its narrative. Robert DeNiro's character, Michael, fights as a Green Beret in Vietnam. But the Green Beret is a significant figure even before Michael and his friends leave Pennsylvania. A uniformed Green Beret wanders into the bar next to the hall where Michael's friends are celebrating a wedding. Michael and two comrades, all scheduled to report for active duty in the army, boozily offer to buy the soldier a drink and ask him, "What's it like over there?" His response is a taciturn, "Fuck it." This scene is important because it presages what will happen to Michael, the only one of the three to wear the green beret and the only one to survive the war intact. The message is that to be a Green Beret is to be a survivor but also to be alienated. As Robin Wood comments, "The Green Beret, though he has returned to America, is no longer 'of' it: totally alienated, he cannot participate, even peripherally, in the celebrations."[13] Even before he earns his own green beret, Michael is shown to be a spiritual brother of the Special Forces soldier. Gilbert Adair notes the similarity, both in title and in characterization, between *The Deer Hunter* and James Fenimore Cooper's nineteenth century novel *The Deerslayer*. Just as Cooper's hero Natty Bumppo is an archetypal frontier hero, so too is Cimino's hero Michael shown to "practise [sic] the frontiersman virtues of independence, self-reliance, and an ease with weapons."[14] Like Bumppo, Michael is "a deerslayer who becomes a manslayer."[15] In joining the Special Forces, Michael becomes only more himself.

In Vietnam, Michael is the one with the skills, nerve, and determination to save himself and his two friends, Steven and Nicky, with whom he is reunited while a prisoner. Michael conceives and executes the daring Russian roulette gambit that allows the Americans to escape from their captors, and Michael carries Steven back to American lines when the latter's legs are broken. Later, Michael returns to Vietnam in an attempt to rescue Nicky from the suicidal madness that has possessed him—an effort that fails.

Thus, the film characterizes Green Berets as highly skilled survivors. But, as shown by the wedding guest early on, the Green Beret returned from the war can never be the same again. Back home, Michael is alienated from virtually everything and everyone. He can no longer hunt deer; the tracking skill is still there, but, when the moment comes to pull the trigger, Michael deliberately fires high and shouts at the deer, "Okay!"

Like John Wayne, Michael Cimino saw the Green Beret as a superb warrior. But Cimino's Special Forces trooper, unlike John Wayne's version, does not seem inclined to sing of "Fighting Soldiers from the Sky." He may manage a verse of "God Bless America," but his heart does not seem to be in it.

A similar version of the Green Beret as damaged hero permeates Francis Ford Coppola's *Apocalypse Now*. The film is, at base, a quest story, and the object of the search undertaken by Captain Willard, portrayed by Martin Sheen, is a renegade Green Beret colonel, Walter E. Kurtz. The colonel has abandoned his command and ensconced himself in Cambodia with an army of Montagnard tribesmen, fighting his own private war against the Viet Cong. Willard is sent to find and kill Kurtz. There is little doubt that the army sees a link between Kurtz's membership in the elite Special Forces and his acting "beyond the pale of any decent human restraint." The general who briefs Willard on his mission says of Kurtz, "He joined the Special Forces, and after that his ideas, his methods, became unsound." Kurtz's separation from civilization seems to be clear even before the viewer sees the barbaric conditions with which Kurtz has surrounded himself. The general calls Kurtz "insane." Later, after reading Kurtz's dossier, Willard concludes, "Kurtz had got off the boat. He'd split from the whole fucking program."

This deliberate alienation puts Kurtz squarely in the backyard of the Frontier Hero. The myth of the Frontier Hero portrays a man not comfortable with civilization, a man whose wilderness skills will ossify if he leaves the woods for any length of time.[16] Daniel Boone, according to legend, regarded civilization as being too close if he could see the chimney smoke coming from the nearest cabin. Thus, the depiction of Kurtz in *Apocalypse Now* is consistent with the legend to which the Green Beret is heir.

But the Frontier Hero is not only rustic—he is also deadly when confronted with enemies. The same is true of Kurtz. As Willard reads in the dossier:

November: Kurtz orders assassination of three Vietnamese men and one woman. Two of the men were colonels in the South Vietnamese army. Enemy activity in his old sector dropped off to nothing. Guess he must have hit the right four people. The army tried one last time to bring him back into the fold, and if he'd pulled over, it all would have been forgotten. But he kept going, and he kept winning it his way. . . . The VC knew his name by now, and they were scared of him.

Kurtz's purposeful violence is shown in chilling contrast to the devastating but random violence employed by other U.S. forces in the film. Colonel Kilgore's air cavalry troopers destroy an entire Vietnamese village largely because a nearby beach promises good surfing. Later, the crew of the navy patrol boat ferrying Willard upriver to find Kurtz conduct a routine search of a *sampan* containing an entire Vietnamese family. The young, jittery crew members mistake sudden movement by a girl on the *sampan* as aggression and open up with automatic weapons, killing everyone but the girl.

This senseless slaughter makes the calculated murders ordered by Kurtz seem rational by comparison. As Terry Christensen noted, "When Willard finally arrives at Kurtz's bizarre encampment, the arguments of the renegade leader and his admirers in favor of their mad methods seem relatively persuasive."[17]

But Willard himself is capable of purposeful violence. The briefing session early in the film reveals that Willard has, on orders, assassinated six people, including a South Vietnamese tax collector. Another example occurs following the massacre of the Vietnamese family on the *sampan* by the nervous navy crewmen. The young girl is the only Vietnamese survivor of the onslaught, and standard operating procedure is, apparently, to take wounded civilians to an aid station. The commander of the patrol boat is preparing to do this—delaying Willard's mission in the process—when Willard, who had no part in the machine-gunning of the *sampan*, deliberately kills the girl with one pistol shot. He then looks at the patrol boat commander and says in a flat voice, "I told you not to stop."

This similarity between Willard and his quarry, Kurtz, is particularly important when one considers that *Willard is himself a Green Beret*. This information is conveyed subtly, so subtly that many critics[18] missed it entirely. Willard does not wear the distinctive headgear of Special Forces and he is described as being part of the 173rd Airborne Regiment. The green beret is worn only by soldiers who are active members of a Special Forces group. But Willard is a graduate of the Special Warfare School, the institution that turns out Green Berets. Reading Kurtz's dossier while on his way upriver, Willard is amazed that Kurtz completed the Special Warfare School at the age of forty-two. Willard's reaction: "The next youngest guy in his class was less than half his age. They must have thought he was some far-out old man, humping it through that course. *I'd done it when I was 19, and it damn near wasted me*" (emphasis added).

Thus, Kurtz and Willard are brothers under the skin. Being Green Berets, both are heroic (if the capacity for purposeful violence is defined as heroism, and the Frontier Hero myth seems to do so). Both are also alienated. Kurtz's alienation has been discussed; even if he is not the monster his Regular Army superiors consider him to be (and the mutilated bodies lying around his Cambodian lair certainly make him look monstrous), he is certainly not part of the army or its war effort. As Willard concludes from Kurtz's dossier: "He could have gone for general; but he went for himself instead."

Willard is also alienated, both from America and from the conventional war effort. His inability to rejoin civilian life in the United States is made clear early. He muses, "When I was here I wanted to be there [back home], and when I was there, all I could think of was getting back into the jungle." Willard is also alienated from the generals in Saigon. As noted, he is an assassin, not a line soldier. And when he arrives at Kurtz's encampment, he is uncertain whether to kill him, join him, or replace him. When Willard finally does decide to kill Kurtz, he does it, but not for the army's reasons. It is almost an act of mercy killing because he knows Kurtz wants someone to "take the pain away." Willard's last line in the film, delivered after Kurtz is dead, shows that his alienation is complete: "They were going to make me a major for this, and I wasn't even in their fucking army anymore."

Thus, two major films about Vietnam portray the figure of the Green Beret as a damaged hero—a man who is highly skilled at the tasks of the frontiersman, but who is also alienated from his own people by the experience of Vietnam. The attitude toward the Green Beret is therefore ambivalent, which may be seen to reflect the attitude of the filmmakers toward the war.

ROCKY CREAMS THE COMMIES: THE RHETORIC OF *RAMBO*

Public taste is said to run in cycles, and it certainly seems true that the ambivalent image of the Green Beret as damaged hero was replaced in the 1980s by a depiction of the Special Forces trooper as Superman, a view that might have made John Wayne proud. The case in point is *Rambo: First Blood II*. Strictly speaking, *Rambo* is not a Vietnam War film, since its action takes place ten years or so after the war's end. But it is clear, according to its writer and star, Sylvester Stallone, that the film depicts Americans with a "chance to win again" in Vietnam.[19]

Although the Rambo of this film has long been separated from the service, the viewer is made aware that he is "a crack veteran of the Green Beret Special Forces."[20] *Rambo* is a sequel to *First Blood*, in which the character's former Special Forces status is made clear, and in both films Richard Crenna plays a major supporting role as Major Sam Trautman, Rambo's former commanding officer in Vietnam. Trautman is still on active duty, and his green headgear is very much in evidence, although, interestingly, Trautman's character does nothing really heroic in either film, except to provide support for Rambo.

To claim that Rambo is a heroic figure may be an exercise in understatement. He parachutes from a plane, withstands torture, escapes his captors, releases U.S. prisoners of war, flies a helicopter, and slaughters innumerable North Vietnamese and Russian soldiers. And the way he does much of this is an interesting reversal of the historical experience of Vietnam for Americans. During the war, the Viet Cong, who usually were outnumbered and outgunned, were successful by virtue of being clever, sneaky, and jungle-wise. In *Rambo*, the American operates alone against a vastly superior force and triumphs by guile and superior guerrilla skills.[21]

That Rambo is able to function so effectively in the jungle is not surprising. He is a Green Beret, and, as such, is a modern incarnation of the Frontier Hero. As Harvey Greenberg writes:

Rambo's . . . character merges with that of another American hero: the virtuous frontiersman, threatened by the corrupting encroachment of civilization. Examples include Uncas of *The Last of the Mohicans*, Natty Bumpo [sic] of *The Deerslayer*, and Tarzan of the Apes. . . . Rambo is half-Indian. His Green Beret training liberated *his* Uncas.[22]

The only major difference between John Wayne's Green Beret and Sylvester Stallone's is that Rambo blames the nation's leaders (both past and present) for the failure to achieve victory. When Trautman offers to effect Rambo's release from prison only if he will undertake a mission in Vietnam, Rambo asks, "Do we get to win this time?" Trautman replies, "This time, it's up to you"—as if the issue were ever in doubt.

CONCLUSION

The Special Forces trooper has been called "the soldier most intimately associated with the Vietnam War in the public mind."[23] He has been portrayed in a number of important films about the war, and the filmmakers' attitude about the war is reflected in the depiction of the Green

Beret himself. *The Green Berets* and *Rambo,* two films showing strong support for America's war effort in Vietnam, portray the Green Beret as an unmitigated hero who uses his considerable skills to achieve victory. Other films that seem more ambivalent about the war, *The Deer Hunter* and *Apocalypse Now*, recognize the Green Beret's formidable aptitudes and abilities but also suggest that the experience of Vietnam leaves no one undamaged—not even the contemporary heir of the Frontier Hero.

NOTES

1. Dan Nimmo and James E. Combs, *Subliminal Politics* (Englewood Cliffs, NJ: Prentice-Hall, 1980), 153.

2. J. Fred MacDonald, *Television and the Red Menace* (New York: Praeger, 1985), 165.

3. Stephen Ausband, *Myth and Meaning, Myth and Order* (Macon, GA: Mercer University Press, 1986), 67–68.

4. John Hellman, *American Myth and the Legacy of Vietnam* (New York: Columbia University Press, 1986), 45.

5. Alasdair Spark, "The Soldier at the Heart of the War: The Myth of the Green Beret in the Popular Culture of the Vietnam War," *Journal of American Studies* 18 (1984): 29–30.

6. Leo Cawley, "Refighting the War: Why the Movies Are in Vietnam," *The Village Voice*, September 8, 1987, 21.

7. Quoted in Lawrence H. Suid, *Guts and Glory: Great American War Movies* (New York: Addison Wesley, 1978), 222.

8. Edward F. Dolan, Jr., *Hollywood Goes to War* (New York: Bison Books, 1985), 116.

9. Cawley, 22.

10. "John Wayne's Green Beret," *The Nation*, December 11, 1967, 614.

11. Spark, 37.

12. Terry Christensen, *Reel Politics* (New York: Basil Blackwell, 1987), 149.

13. Robin Wood, *Hollywood from Vietnam to Reagan* (New York: Columbia University Press, 1986), 284–285.

14. Gilbert Adair, *Vietnam on Film* (New York: Proteus Publishing, 1981), 135.

15. David Ayeen, "Eastern Western," *Film Quarterly* 32 (1979): 17.

16. Hellman, 55–56.

17. Christensen, 154.

18. Spark, 43.

19. Fred Bruning, "A Nation Succumbs to Rambomania," *McLean's*, July 29, 1985, 7.

20. Richard Zoglin, "An Outbreak of Rambomania," *Time*, June 24, 1985, 72.

21. Zoglin, 72.

22. Harvey R. Greenberg, "Dangerous Recuperations: *Red Dawn, Rambo*, and the New Decaturism," *Journal of Popular Film and Television* 15 (1987): 68.

23. Spark, 29.

Chapter Eleven

Apocalypse Now: A Burkeian Analysis of Cinematic Rhetoric

The notion that film can be rhetorical is not new. By what a filmmaker includes or excludes, by tone, by characterization, by lighting, by perspective and soundtrack, he or she can make statements that may have a persuasive effect on an audience. This is easiest to achieve in a documentary,[1] but it is equally possible to take a rhetorical perspective in a film based in fiction.[2]

Any attempt to portray the Vietnam War on film must necessarily have rhetorical elements. The war itself has been the subject of so much rhetoric, both prowar and antiwar, and of such strong emotion that it is probably impossible to make a completely neutral and objective film about the Vietnam conflict. Thus, *The Green Berets* is generally considered a prowar film,[3] and *The Boys in Company C* is seen as an antiwar film.[4]

Clearly, Francis Ford Coppola's film *Apocalypse Now* may be considered an antiwar statement.[5] Of somewhat more interest to the scholar and the subject of this chapter is the question of how Coppola[6] made various antiwar arguments in the film. Answering this question involves, in effect, analyzing Coppola's rhetorical techniques.

One of the more interesting ways to analyze rhetorical techniques has been developed from the writings of literary critic and philosopher Kenneth Burke. Arguably one of the most influential men of letters of the twentieth century,[7] Burke described communication as "the drama of human relations."[8] He believes that human communication can best be understood when viewed through the perspective of dramatic (or theatrical) conventions. From this notion has arisen what is called the Burkeian pentad: five elements of drama that can be employed to discuss human communication. The elements are Act (what is done), Agent (who performs the Act), Agency (the means or instrument used to perform the Act), Scene (the place and time wherein the Act takes place), and Purpose (the reason the Agent undertakes the Act).[9]

Employed as a tool of rhetorical criticism, the Burkeian pentad allows the critic to determine the underlying meaning that may exist in a message, the "drama" being presented to the audience by the rhetor. Critics have used the Burkeian pentad to analyze rhetoric in many of its forms, including public speaking,[10] political debates,[11] and theatre,[12] and even a mass murder and suicide.[13]

As noted, a film can also be an example of rhetoric, which brings us to *Apocalypse Now*. To discuss Francis Ford Coppola's rhetorical vision in the film, it is necessary to construct several pentads.[14]

The first pentad contains the following elements:

Agent:	U.S. Army
Agency:	Conventional warfare
Act:	Senseless violence
Scene:	America (psychologically)
Purpose:	Victory

This pentad focuses on the U.S. military force in Vietnam as Agent (although the U.S. military presence in Vietnam included army, navy, air force, and marine units, for brevity these will be subsumed under the heading "U.S. Army"; then, too, *Apocalypse Now* focuses almost exclusively on army units). The Agency (or tool) employed by the army is conventional warfare, which assumes particular importance when contrasted with the other pentads developed later. The Scene, the crucial element, is not, as one might expect, Vietnam—it is America. This does not mean that Coppola portrays U.S. soldiers conducting firefights in the streets of Dayton, Ohio. Rather, he is saying very clearly that the Americans in Vietnam are still in America *psychologically*. They fight in an Americanized Vietnam, a false Vietnam, a Vietnam removed from reality. Many examples of this Americanized Vietnam appear in the film: the lavish roast beef dinner during which Captain Willard, the protagonist and narrator, receives his orders; the T-bone steaks and beer that Colonel Kilgore's airmobile troops feast on between attacks; the American troops surfing during a firefight on a nearby beach; and the USO show that Willard encounters at a remote outpost, complete with go-go dancing Playboy Playmates. As Gilbert Adair writes in *Vietnam on Film*, "The Southeast Asia of *Apocalypse Now* is also a vision of America: the whole Kilgore set-up, the California-style surfing and beach barbeque, the disc-jockeys on Saigon radio and the enormous, incandescent supply depot."[15] As Willard puts it, "They tried to make it just like home." The film implies very strongly that, because these yokels haven't really adapted to Vietnam but have tried to make Vietnam adapt to them, they cannot be successful in fighting the war. This ties in with what Coppola shows as the Act in this pentad: senseless violence. The Americans are very good at killing people, the film says, but they are neither efficient nor selective. Kilgore's airmobile cavalrymen destroy a Vietnamese village because the nearby beach promises good surfing. Later, the patrol boat crew (described by Willard as "rock and rollers with one foot in their graves") taking Willard to Cambodia stops a Vietnamese *sampan* for a routine check despite Willard's advice to keep going. When a teenage girl makes a sudden move toward a basket, the crew kills everyone on board the *sampan* except her. As it turns out, the girl was reaching for a puppy in the basket; no weapons are found on the *sampan*.

The hypocrisy of this American approach to waging war is portrayed several times in the film. Early on, the general who briefs Willard on his mission says of Kurtz, "He's out there operating without any decent restraint, totally beyond the pale of any acceptable human conduct." The irony of these words becomes evident, especially after Kilgore destroys the village so he and his men can surf, and Willard comments directly, "If that's how Kilgore fought the war, I wondered what they [the military] had against Kurtz." The Purpose of the army in Vietnam, as depicted by this pentad, is to win the war, a Purpose shared by others, as will be seen, but Willard doesn't think they have much chance: "The war was being run by a bunch of four-star clowns who were going to end up giving the whole circus away."

The second pentad looks like this:

Agent:	Viet Cong
Agency:	Guerrilla warfare
Act:	Purposeful violence
Scene:	Vietnam (literally and psychologically)
Purpose:	Victory

The Scene is again the most important element in this pentad. The Scene in which Coppola shows the Viet Cong operating is the real Vietnam, the real jungle. Viet Cong don't surf, as Colonel Kilgore notes, they don't have beach parties, nor do voluptuous maidens descend from the sky to titillate them. As Willard observes following the gaudy USO show in the middle of the jungle: "Charlie didn't get much USO. He was dug in too deep or moving too fast. His idea of great R & R [rest and recuperation] was cold rice and a little rat meat. He had only two ways home—death or victory." And as Willard—and, through him, Coppola—makes clear from the start, the Viet Cong guerrilla's connection with the jungle gives him the strength and will to fight a jungle war; the Americanized Vietnam only enervates the Americans. Willard says, "Every minute I stay in this room [in Saigon] I get weaker, and every minute Charlie squats in the bush he gets stronger."

The Act performed by the Viet Cong is purposeful violence, in contrast to the mindless slaughter perpetrated by the Americans. Although there is virtually no combat between Americans and Viet Cong or North Vietnamese army depicted in the film, the Viet Cong are nonetheless discussed at length. When Willard finally finds him, Kurtz speaks openly of how he came to understand and admire the Viet Cong and describes an incident when he was still part of the U.S. Army's war effort. He and his Special Forces team had entered a village and vaccinated all the children there against polio. After the Americans left, the Viet Cong came in and cut off every arm bearing a vaccination mark. Kurtz admits that his initial reactions were rage, revulsion, and horror, but eventually he came to regard this act of terrorism as a work of "genius." He seems to be saying that the Viet Cong knew exactly what they wanted to accomplish, and they had the will to do what they saw as necessary, unpleasant though it may have been. Of course, the Viet Cong, from their perspective, are operating with the same Purpose as the Americans: to achieve victory. But the rhetorical vision of the film (aided by historical hindsight) says the Viet Cong are more likely than the Americans to achieve their purpose. As Kurtz tells Willard, "If we had ten divisions of those men [the Viet Cong who cut off the children's arms], our troubles here would be over very quickly."

Kurtz deserves a pentad of his own containing the following elements:

Agent: Kurtz
Agency: Guerrilla warfare
Act: Purposeful violence
Scene: Vietnam (literally and psychologically)
Purpose: Victory

Kurtz's Purpose, like that of every other Agent, is to win the war, or, at least, to win his portion of it. Although Kurtz is an American, his Agency is guerrilla warfare, not the conventional approach employed by the U.S. Army. He has a private army of Montagnards, Vietnamese hill people—an ethnic minority in Vietnam, who mostly live in the Central Highlands—who, as an army colonel puts it, "worship the man, and will carry out any order, no matter how insane." The Special Forces had trained Montagnards and used them as guerrillas against the Viet Cong, but Kurtz has taken the Special Forces mission a step further. Operating out of Cambodia, he is waging his own war against the Communist forces and, apparently, winning. The army's dossier on Kurtz reports:

November. Kurtz orders assassination of three Vietnamese men and one woman. Two of the men were colonels in the South Vietnamese army. Enemy activity in his old sector dropped off to nothing. Guess he must have hit the right four people. The army tried one last time to bring him back into the fold, and if he'd pulled over, it all would have been forgotten. But he kept going. And he kept winning it his way.... The VC knew his name by now, and they were scared of him.

Kurtz and his Montagnards are winning while the infinitely larger and better-equipped American army is losing. Kurtz wins because of the Scene in which he operates, both psychologically and literally: the real jungle, the real Vietnam, just like the Viet Cong. The American generals eat roast beef in cozy quarters in Saigon and elsewhere. Kurtz and his private army live in a series of caves in Cambodia. He is in the jungle literally, which makes a difference, but he is also in the jungle psychologically, which is where it really counts. As Willard muses while contemplating his plan to kill Kurtz, "Even the jungle wanted him dead, and that's who he really took his orders from, anyway."

Thus, the Act, as undertaken by Kurtz, is the same as that performed by the Viet Cong: purposeful violence. Kurtz doesn't go hunting mice with a cannon, like the U.S. Army. If four people are spies, then those are the four people who die. When Kurtz's army goes to war, it kills North Vietnamese and Viet Cong—it doesn't bomb the wrong village by mistake. That is why Kurtz is so successful, and also why he scares the hell out of the American army: he lives in the Viet Cong's world, and he fights them with their own weapons.

The final pentad focuses on Willard, and its elements are as follows:

Agent:	Willard
Agency:	Guerrilla warfare
Act:	Purposeful violence
Scene:	Vietnam (literally and psychologically)
Purpose:	To kill Kurtz

Although Willard's mission in *Apocalypse Now* is assassination, he is clearly a master of guerrilla warfare. Indeed, assassination is an integral part of guerrilla warfare. Early in the film, Willard is described as liking to "work alone," and it is suggested that he has assassinated a Vietnamese tax collector. Although Willard wears the uniform, he is not really part of the army as depicted in the film. Nor does he operate in the same Scene as the army. As with Kurtz and the Viet Cong, Willard's

Scene is the real Vietnam, the real jungle. At one point, Willard refers to his last leave back in the states: "When I was here I wanted to be there, and when I was there, all I could think of was getting back to the jungle."

Willard's Act is also similar to those of Kurtz and the Viet Cong. All three are capable of purposeful violence. This is illustrated, of course, in Willard's murder of Kurtz, but a better example occurs earlier in the film, during the incident between the nervous patrol boat crew and the *sampan*. The only survivor is a young girl. The commander of the patrol boat prepares to take her to an aid station, following standard American procedure—thus delaying the mission—when Willard, who had no part in machine gunning the *sampan*, deliberately shoots the girl dead. He says in a flat voice to the commander, "I told you not to stop."

The contrast is obvious, and chilling. The "rock and rollers" on the boat open up with machine guns for any reason but then want to delay their mission by taking their victims to the hospital. Willard, like Kurtz, does not kill people by mistake. When Willard kills, he does it for what he regards as a good reason. He is, of course, the perfect man to go after Kurtz, and it may be that the generals in Saigon weren't so dumb, after all. They followed the principle embodied in the maxim "Set a thief to catch a thief."

Interestingly, Willard's motivation has undergone a change by the climax of the film. He starts intending to carry out the army's mission. But by the end, he seems to be working for Kurtz, sensing that Kurtz wants to die, wants someone to take the pain away. Even calling for the air strike to destroy the Montagnards, as he does at the end, seems to fulfill Kurtz's last wishes. After he has killed Kurtz, Willard finds Kurtz's note: "Drop the bomb—exterminate them all."

Thus, the rhetorical vision created by Francis Ford Coppola and others in *Apocalypse Now* is that there is a strong relationship between environment and action (what Burke would call Scene and Act) and between action and outcome. The Americans, as depicted in the film, have never really left America. Or, to be more precise, they have tried to recreate America in Vietnam, complete with surfing, barbeques, and go-go girls. As a result, despite their immense destructive capability, they are essentially incapable of winning a jungle war. On the other hand, the Viet Cong, Kurtz, and Willard have all adapted to the jungle and its hardships and have thus become effective guerrilla fighters. The film says that because those Americans who did adapt to the jungle were either considered outcasts (like Kurtz) or became alienated themselves (like Willard at the end), America had no chance to win the war in Vietnam.

Apocalypse Now is a complex, multilayered film, and this chapter is not intended to be an exhaustive critique of it. But it is hoped that this application of Kenneth Burke's notion of the dramatistic pentad illuminates the rhetorical vision contained in the film and serves as a starting point for others to apply Burke's theories to film criticism.

NOTES

1. Thomas W. Benson, "The Rhetorical Structure of Frederick Wiseman's *High School*," *Communication Monographs* 47 (November 1980): 233–261.

2. See Martin Medhurst, "*Hiroshima, Mon Amour*: From Iconography to Rhetoric," *Quarterly Journal of Speech* 68 (November 1982): 345–370. See also Janice Hocker Rushing and Thomas S. Frentz, " 'The Deer Hunter': Rhetoric of the Warrior," *Quarterly Journal of Speech* 66 (December 1980): 392–406.

3. Gilbert Adair, *Vietnam on Film: From the Green Berets to Apocalypse Now* (New York: Proteus Books, 1981), 40.

4. Ibid., 120.

5. Ibid., 150–151.

6. I am not a devotee of the "Auteur Theory" of filmmaking. For simplicity's sake, however, when reference to the people who made *Apocalypse Now* is required, "Coppola" is used. Two other people who made significant contributions to the aspects of the film studied in this essay are screenwriter John Milius and Michael Herr, who wrote the voice-over narration spoken in the film by Willard (Martin Sheen).

7. For some indication of Burke's impact on modern criticism, see William H. Ruekert, ed., *Critical Responses to Kenneth Burke* (Minneapolis: University of Minnesota Press, 1969). See also Hayden White and Margaret Brose, eds., *Representing Kenneth Burke* (Baltimore: Johns Hopkins University Press, 1982).

8. See William H. Ruekert, *Kenneth Burke and the Drama of Human Relations*, 2d ed. (Berkeley: University of California Press, 1982).

9. Kenneth Burke, *A Grammar of Motives* (Berkeley: University of California Press, 1969), xv–xxiii.

10. David A. Ling, "A Pentadic Analysis of Senator Edward Kennedy's Address to the People of Massachusetts, July 25, 1969," *Central States Speech Journal* 21 (Summer 1970): 81–86.

11. Jane N. Blankenship, Marlene G. Fine, and Leslie K. Davis, "The 1980 Republican Primary Debates: The Transformation of Actor to Scene," *Quarterly Journal of Speech* 69 (February 1983): 25–36.

12. S. John Macksoud and Ross Altman, "Voices in Opposition: A Burkeian Rhetoric of *Saint Joan*," *Quarterly Journal of Speech* 57 (April 1971): 140–146.

13. Jeanne Y. Fisher, "A Burkeian Analysis of the Rhetorical Dimensions of a Multiple Murder and Suicide," *Quarterly Journal of Speech* 60 (April 1974): 175–189.

14. Quotations from *Apocalypse Now* used in this chapter were obtained by using a videocassette of the film, taking notes of relevant passages, and then replaying those segments to check the accuracy of the notes.

15. Adair, 155.

Appendix: The Vietnam War: A Political, Military, and Rhetorical Chronology

1954

April
: President Dwight Eisenhower gives a speech using the domino theory for the first time to explain the threat of Communist expansion.

May
: The U.S. government refuses calls for direct military aid after French troops at Dien Bien Phu are defeated.

July
: An end to Vietnamese fighting is negotiated by an international agreement in Geneva.

: With U.S. help, Ngo Dinh Diem becomes premier in the South with Saigon as capital.

: The North is ruled by Ho Chi Minh.

1955
: American advisers are sent for the first time to train the South Vietnamese army.

: On a visit to Vietnam, Vice President Richard Nixon proclaims the war a reaction by democracy to the threat of Communism.

1957
: South Vietnam experiences terrorism targeting President Diem's police and American aides.

May
: President Diem is welcomed in Washington as a hero by President Eisenhower.

1959

April 4
: President Eisenhower promises to keep South Vietnam a distinct country.

1960

November   John F. Kennedy is elected president of the United States.

1961

January 21   John F. Kennedy is inaugurated president and promises to "pay any price, bear any burden" in defense of freedom.

February   President Kennedy lets it be known that American advisers will defend themselves if attacked.

March   Kennedy sends Marines to Thailand and says they may intervene in Laos if necessary.

                    President Kennedy sends 1,000 additional advisers after General Maxwell Taylor requests a 10,000-man force in Vietnam.

June   At a Vienna summit, neutralization of Laos is agreed on by President Kennedy and Premier Khrushchev. The Soviet leader, however, also tells Kennedy that he will aid "wars of national liberation" in Third World countries.

1963

November 2   President Diem is overthrown in a coup and murdered. The Kennedy administration, aware of the impending revolt, does nothing to stop it.

November 22   President Kennedy, on a visit to Dallas, Texas, is assassinated; Lyndon Johnson assumes the office of president.

1964

August 2   In the Gulf of Tonkin, off the coast of North Vietnam, the USS Maddox is allegedly attacked by North Vietnamese patrol boats.

August 7   The Gulf of Tonkin Resolution is passed by the U.S. Senate; the president is thereby authorized to take whatever steps necessary to deal with Communist aggression.

October   At the University of California at Berkeley, the first protests against the Vietnam War take place.

November 2   President Johnson defeats Republican Barry Goldwater to win a full term as president.

November   First significant attack on U.S. forces in Vietnam takes place when Viet Cong shell Bien Hoa.

1965

March   First commitment of U.S. combat troops takes place when Marines land at Da Nang.

	Widespread bombing of North Vietnam begins.
April 17	First major antiwar protest, sponsored by Students for a Democratic Society (SDS), occurs in the nation's capital.
May 15	"Teach-ins" are held on campuses nationwide, offering information and opinions to contradict the Johnson administration's position on Vietnam.
May	The first U.S. Army troops arrive in Vietnam.
October 15–16	Protests against the war take place in forty U.S. cities. Burning draft cards as a symbol of opposition occurs for the first time.
1966	The U.S. Senate holds televised hearings on the administration's role in Vietnam.
April 7	In a major policy address at Johns Hopkins University, President Johnson explains and defends his commitments to Vietnam.
November	Nationwide protests against the war occur under the aegis of the New Mobe coalition.
1967	
March	Reverend Martin Luther King, Jr., an erstwhile supporter of President Johnson, speaks out against the war.
October	In a series of demonstrations, more than 100,000 people protest at the Pentagon. Hundreds are arrested.
October	Rev. Phillip Berrigan and the other "Baltimore Four" pour blood over draft files to protest the war.
1968	
January 3	Senator Eugene McCarthy announces that he will challenge President Johnson for the Democratic presidential nomination.
January 30	Tet Offensive begins as Viet Cong forces launch simultaneous surprise attacks on cities and military bases throughout South Vietnam.
February 27	In a CBS television special, Walter Cronkite states that the Vietnam War is probably unwinnable and that the United States should negotiate.
March 12	President Johnson is almost beaten by Senator Eugene McCarthy in the New Hampshire primary. For an incumbent president, this is regarded as a serious setback.

March 16	Senator Robert Kennedy states that he, too, will seek the Democratic nomination.
	Troops from the U.S. Army's Americal Division, under the command of Lt. William Calley, massacre Vietnamese civilians at the village of My Lai.
March 31	President Johnson announces on nationwide television that he will neither seek nor accept renomination as president.
April 23–26	Columbia University's SDS chapter occupies several campus buildings in protest against the war; riots follow police efforts to remove them.
May 17	The Revs. Daniel and Phillip Berrigan and the other "Catonsville Nine" burn draft files and are arrested.
June 6	Senator Robert Kennedy is assassinated.
July	Chicago hosts the Democratic National Convention, which nominates Vice President Hubert Humphrey. Massive demonstrations take place throughout the period, culminating in a "police riot" in which many protesters and police are injured.
September	"Milwaukee Fourteen" burn draft files and are arrested.
September 26	"Chicago Eight" (later "Chicago Seven") conspiracy trial begins.
October 7	"Catonsville Nine" trial begins in Baltimore.
October 8–11	Weathermen "Days of Rage" protest occurs in Chicago.

1969

January 22	Richard Nixon is inaugurated as president.
May 20	Paris peace talks begin.
July 8	President Nixon announces the first withdrawal of American forces from Vietnam.
October 15	The first National Moratorium Day; demonstrations take place in cities and on campuses across the country.
November 3	President Nixon's "silent majority" speech.
November 15	Second Moratorium Day demonstrations.

1970

March 6	A Manhattan townhouse being used as a Weathermen bomb factory blows up, killing three members of the organization.

April 30   U.S. and South Vietnamese forces invade Cambodia to attack North Vietnamese sanctuaries there.

May 4   Ohio National Guard troops fire on protesting students at Kent State University, killing four.

1971

May   Last significant antiwar protests take place.

June 13   The *New York Times* begins publishing the *Pentagon Papers,* a secret government history of the war.

1972

February 21   President Nixon visits the People's Republic of China, seeking to improve relations between the two countries.

June 22   An attempted burglary of the Democratic National Committee in Washington's Watergate building begins a scandal that will ultimately end President Nixon's Administration.

October 28   Secretary of State Henry Kissinger announces that "peace is at hand" in the Vietnam War.

November 7   In a landslide victory, President Nixon defeats Senator George McGovern to win reelection.

1973

January   The U.S. Selective Service system ceases operation; no more men are drafted into military service.

March   The last U.S. combat troops leave Vietnam.

1974

August 9   President Nixon resigns in the face of possible impeachment; Vice President Gerald R. Ford assumes the office of president.

September 16   President Ford offers conditional clemency to military deserters and draft dodgers living outside the United States.

1975

April 30   Saigon falls to the North Vietnamese army; South Vietnam ceases to exist as a political entity; the Vietnam War ends.

Selected Bibliography

Rather than recycle all of the endnotes from all the chapters, I have listed below the sources that I find most important, useful, and/or interesting for various aspects of the Vietnam War and its rhetoric. Although most of the sources listed herein appeared in the endnotes for one or more chapters, a few do not. With a few exceptions, the organization followed reflects the order of the chapters, although some chapters are collapsed together for the sake of simplicity.

CULTURAL HISTORIES OF THE VIETNAM WAR

Baritz, Loren. *Backfire*. New York: William Morrow, 1985.

Gibson, James William. *The Perfect War*. Boston: Atlantic Monthly Press, 1986.

Morris, Richard, and Peter Ehrenhaus, eds. *Cultural Legacies of Vietnam*. Norwood, NJ: Ablex, 1990.

Rowe, John Carlos, and Rick Berg. *The Vietnam War and American Culture*. New York: Columbia University Press, 1991.

Shafer, D. Michael, ed. *The Legacy: The Vietnam War and the American Imagination*. Boston: Beacon Press, 1990.

HISTORIES OF THE 1960s

Albert, Judith Clavir, and Stewart Edward Albert. *The Sixties Papers*. New York: Praeger, 1984.

Blum, John Morton. *Years of Discord*. New York: W. W. Norton, 1991.

Collier, Peter, and David Horowitz. *Destructive Generation*. New York: Summit Books, 1990.

Gitlin, Todd. *The Sixties: Years of Hope, Days of Rage*. New York: Bantam Books, 1987.

McQuaid, Kim. *The Anxious Years*. New York: Basic Books, 1989.

Morgan, Edward P. *The 60s Experience*. Philadelphia, PA: Temple University Press, 1991.

Morrison, Joan, and Robert K. Morrison. *From Camelot to Kent State*. New York: Times Books, 1987.

Viorst, Milton. *Fire in the Streets*. New York: Bantam Books, 1979.

THE DOMINO THEORY

Arnold, James R. *The First Domino*. New York: William Morrow, 1991.

"The Falling Dominos." *Newsweek*, October 27, 1969, 24.

Olson, James S., and Randy Roberts. *Where the Domino Fell*. New York: St. Martin's Press, 1991.

Silverman, Jerry Mark. "The Domino Theory: Alternatives to a Self-Fulfilling Prophecy." *Asian Survey* 15 (1975): 915–939.

JOHN F. KENNEDY AND THE GREEN BERETS

Cockerham, William C. "Green Berets and the Symbolic Meaning of Heroism." *Urban Life* 8 (1979): 94–113.

Cohen, Eliot A. *Commandos and Politicians*. Cambridge, MA: Harvard University Center for International Affairs, 1978.

Hellman, John. *American Myth and the Legacy of Vietnam*. New York: Columbia University Press, 1986.

Rust, William J. *Kennedy in Vietnam*. New York: Charles Scribner's Sons, 1985.

Spark, Alasdair. " 'The Soldier at the Heart of the War': The Myth of the Green Beret in the Popular Culture of the Vietnam Era." *Journal of American Studies* 18 (1984): 29–48.

LYNDON JOHNSON AND THE TET OFFENSIVE

Cherwitz, Richard A. "Lyndon Johnson and the 'Crisis' of Tonkin Gulf: A President's Justification for War." *Western Journal of Speech Communication* 42 (1978): 93–104.

Logue, Cal M., and John H. Patton. "From Ambiguity to Dogma: The Rhetorical Symbols of Lyndon B. Johnson on Vietnam." *The Southern Speech Communication Journal* 47 (1982): 315–321.

Oberdorfer, Don. *Tet!* Garden City, NY: Doubleday, 1971.

Schandler, Herbert Y. *The Unmaking of a President*. Princeton, NJ: Princeton University Press, 1977.

Smith, F. Michael. "Rhetorical Implications of the 'Aggression' Thesis on the Johnson Administration's Vietnam Argumentation." *Central States Speech Journal* 23 (1972): 217–224.

Turner, Kathleen J. *Lyndon Johnson's Dual War*. Chicago: University of Chicago Press, 1985.

RICHARD NIXON AND THE SILENT MAJORITY

Bochin, Hal W. *Richard Nixon: Rhetorical Strategist.* Westport, CT: Greenwood Press, 1990.

Campbell, Karlyn Kohrs. *Critiques of Contemporary Rhetoric.* Belmont, CA: Wadsworth Publishing, 1972.

Hill, Forbes. "Conventional Wisdom—Traditional Form: The President's Message of November 2, 1969." *Quarterly Journal of Speech* 58 (1972): 373–386.

King, Andrew A., and Floyd Douglas Anderson. "Nixon, Agnew, and the 'Silent Majority': A Case Study in the Rhetoric of Polarization." *Western Speech* 35 (1971): 243–255.

Newman, Robert P. "Under the Veneer: Nixon's Vietnam Speech of November 3, 1969." *Quarterly Journal of Speech* 56 (1970): 113–128.

Reich, Robert B. *Tales of a New America.* New York: Vintage Books, 1987.

Rosenberg, Milton J., Sidney Verba, and Phillip E. Converse. *Vietnam and the Silent Majority: The Dove's Guide.* New York: Harper & Row, 1970.

Stelzner, Herman. "The Quest Story and Nixon's November 3, 1969 Address." *Quarterly Journal of Speech* 57 (1971): 163–172.

DANIEL BERRIGAN AND THE CATHOLIC ULTRA-RESISTANCE

Berrigan, Daniel. *America Is Hard to Find.* Garden City, NY: Doubleday, 1972.

Berrigan, Daniel. *No Bars to Manhood.* New York: Bantam Books, 1971.

Casey, William VanEtten, ed. *The Berrigans.* New York: Avon Books, 1971.

Curtis, Richard. *The Berrigan Brothers.* New York: Hawthorn Books, 1974.

Gray, Francine du Plessix. *Divine Disobedience: Profiles in Catholic Radicalism.* New York: Alfred A. Knopf, 1970.

Halpert, Stephen, and Tom Murray. *Witness of the Berrigans.* Garden City, NY: Doubleday, 1972.

Labrie, Ross. *The Writings of Daniel Berrigan.* Lanham, MD: University Press of America, 1989.

Meconis, Charles A. *With Clumsy Grace: The American Catholic Left 1961–1975.* New York: The Seabury Press, 1979.

Patton, John H. "Rhetoric at Catonsville: Daniel Berrigan, Conscience, and Image Alteration." *Today's Speech* 23 (1975): 3–12.

STUDENTS FOR A DEMOCRATIC SOCIETY

Adelson, Alan. *SDS: A Profile.* New York: Charles Scribner's Sons, 1972.

Gitlin, Todd. *The Whole World Is Watching.* Berkeley, CA: University of California Press, 1980.

Heath, G. Louis. *Vandals in the Bomb Factory: The History and Literature of the Students for a Democratic Society.* Metuchen, NJ: The Scarecrow Press, 1976.

Miller, James. *"Democracy Is in the Streets": From Port Huron to the Siege of Chicago.* New York: Simon & Schuster, 1987.

Sale, Kirkpatrick. *SDS.* New York: Random House, 1973.

THE WEATHERMEN

Collier, Peter, and David Horowitz. *Destructive Generation*. New York: Summit Books, 1990.
Daniels, Stuart. "The Weathermen." *Government and Opposition* 9 (1974): 430–459.
Jacobs, Harold, ed. *Weatherman*. New York: Ramparts Press, 1970.
Kifner, John. "Vandals in the Mother Country." *The New York Times Magazine*, January 4, 1970, 14–16; 124–128.
Miller, Frederick D. "The End of SDS and the Emergence of Weatherman: Demise through Success." In *Social Movements of the Sixties and Seventies*, ed. Jo Freeman. New York: Longman, 1983.
Sale, Kirkpatrick. *SDS*. New York: Random House, 1973.

THE ANTIWAR MOVEMENT

Berkowitz, William R. "The Impact of Anti-Vietnam Demonstrations upon National Public Opinion and Military Indicators." *Social Science Research* 2 (1973): 1–14.
Burstein, Paul, and William Freudenburg. "Changing Public Policy: The Impact of Public Opinion, Anti-War Demonstrations, and War Costs on Senate Voting on Vietnam War Motions." *American Journal of Sociology* 84 (1978): 99–122.
Fisher, Randall M. *Rhetoric and American Democracy*. Lanham, MD: University Press of America, 1985.
Gitlin, Todd. *The Whole World Is Watching*. Berkeley, CA: University of California Press, 1980.
Kendrick, Alexander. *The Wound Within: America in the Vietnam Years, 1945–1974*. Boston: Little, Brown, 1974.
Mueller, John E. *War, Presidents, and Public Opinion*. New York: John Wiley & Sons, 1973.
Schreiber, E. M. "American Politics and the Vietnam Issue: Demonstrations, Votes, and Public Opinion." *Politics* 10 (1975): 207–209.
Schreiber, E. M. "Anti-War Demonstrations and American Public Opinion on the War in Vietnam." *British Journal of Sociology* 27 (1976): 225–236.
Schuman, Howard. "Two Sources of Anti-War Sentiment in America." *American Journal of Sociology* 78 (1972): 513–536.
Small, Melvin. *Johnson, Nixon, and the Doves*. New Brunswick, NJ: Rutgers University Press, 1988.
Windt, Theodore Otto, Jr. *Presidents and Protesters: Political Rhetoric in the 1960s*. Tuscaloosa, AL: University of Alabama Press, 1990.
Zaroulis, Nancy, and Gerald Sullivan. *Who Spoke Up?* Garden City, NY: Doubleday, 1984.

DOONESBURY

Alter, Jonathan. "Real Life with Garry Trudeau." *Newsweek*, October 15, 1990, 60–66.

"Doonesbury: Drawing and Quartering for Fun and Profit." *Time*, February 9, 1976, 57–66.

Trudeau, G. B. *The Doonesbury Chronicles*. New York: Holt, Rinehart, and Winston, 1975.

Turner, Kathleen J. "Comic Strips: A Rhetorical Perspective." *Central States Speech Journal* 28 (1977): 24–35.

VIETNAM WAR FILMS

Adair, Gilbert. *Vietnum on Film*. New York: Proteus Publishing, 1981.

Anderegg, Michael, ed. *Inventing Vietnam*. Philadelphia, PA: Temple University Press, 1991.

Auster, Albert, and Leonard Quart. *How the War Was Remembered*. New York: Praeger Publishers, 1988.

Greenburg, Harvey R. "Dangerous Recuperations: *Red Dawn*, *Rambo*, and the New Decaturism." *Journal of Popular Film and Television* 15 (1987): 60–70.

Pittmar, Linda, and Gene Michaud, eds. *From Hanoi to Hollywood*. New Brunswick, NJ: Rutgers University Press, 1990.

Index

About the Author

J. JUSTIN GUSTAINIS is Associate Professor of Communication at the State University of New York at Plattsburgh. He has written numerous journal articles in the field of political rhetoric and is currently working on a book-length study of the rhetoric of Jimmy Carter.